Praise for

CHAKRA *Awakening*

Get out your highlighter! Margaret Ann Lembo's wonderful book is filled with profound ancient wisdom, but at the same time it's overflowing with usable and transformational information. It's a great resource for anyone's library. This book can truly help you to balance all of your chakras (and your life) with ease and joy!

—Denise Linn, bestselling author of *Sacred Space*

Chakra Awakening brings the ancient knowledge and sacred use of crystals and gemstones into present-day focus. This wonderful book is a very useful reference for anyone interested in the healing power of gemstones.

—Caroline M. Sutherland, author of *The Body "Knows"*

Filled with valuable information for personal growth, spiritual practices, and Margaret's unique insights and warm humor, her crystalline and loving intent shines through the many facets of guidance offered in what I hope is the first of other books of hers to come in the future.

—Josie Ravenwing, author of *The Book of Miracles*

A straightforward, far-reaching, and complete guide that clearly takes you on the wondrous and magical path of personal evolution in this lifetime. Read this book and follow it! Be prepared to take off with this flight manual for your spiritual ascent.

—James Wanless, creator of Voyager Tarot and author of *Intuition @ Work*

A treasure trove of healing wisdom imbued with practical guidance, humor, and expansive insight. All the tools to heal yourself and others are covered, including quartz crystals, gemstones, aromatherapy, herbs and flower essences, structured water, angels, spirit guides, and more. I love this book—you will, too!

—Melissa Littlefield Applegate, author of *The Egyptian Book of Life*

CHAKRA
Awakening

About the Author

Margaret Ann Lembo is a spiritual practitioner and owner of The Crystal Garden, a spiritual center and gift shop. For more than twenty years, she has led workshops and classes around the country. Her audio CDs (guided meditations and more) are distributed nationally. She is also the president of the Coalition of Visionary Resources (COVR). Visit her online at www.margaretannlembo.com.

To Write to the Author

If you wish to contact the author or would like more information about this book, please write to the author in care of Llewellyn Worldwide and we will forward your request. Both the author and the publisher appreciate hearing from you and learning of your enjoyment of this book and how it has helped you. Llewellyn Worldwide cannot guarantee that every letter written to the author can be answered, but all will be forwarded. Please write to:

Margaret Ann Lembo
c/o Llewellyn Worldwide
2143 Wooddale Drive
Woodbury, MN 55125-2989

Please enclose a self-addressed stamped envelope for reply,
or $1.00 to cover costs. If outside the U.S.A., enclose
an international postal reply coupon.

Many of Llewellyn's authors have websites with additional information and resources. For more information, please visit our website at:

www.llewellyn.com

CHAKRA
Awakening

TRANSFORM YOUR REALITY USING
CRYSTALS, COLOR, AROMATHERAPY &
THE POWER OF POSITIVE THOUGHT

MARGARET ANN LEMBO

Llewellyn Publications
Woodbury, Minnesota

First Edition
Fifth Printing, 2014

Cover design by Ellen Lawson
Cover images: flower © iStockphoto.com/Dmitriy Shironosov;
    background © Valueline/PunchStock
Color photographs of gemstones © Margaret Ann Lembo
Interior illustration by Llewellyn Art Department
Editing by Laura Graves

Llewellyn is a registered trademark of Llewellyn Worldwide Ltd.

Library of Congress Cataloging-in-Publication Data
Lembo, Margaret Ann, 1957–
   Chakra awakening : transform your reality using crystals, color, aromatherapy & the power of positive thought / Margaret Ann Lembo. – 1st ed.
       p. cm.
   Includes bibliographical references (p.   ) and index.
   ISBN 978-0-7387-1485-1
   1. Chakras. 2. Self-realization. I. Title.
   BF1442.C53L46 2011
   131—dc22
                                    2010051461

Llewellyn Publications
A Division of Llewellyn Worldwide Ltd.
2143 Wooddale Drive
Woodbury, MN 55125-2989
www.llewellyn.com

Printed in the United States of America

To Ted Andrews
Thank you for opening the door to Llewellyn Worldwide
and the publication of my first book.
I am grateful for your endorsement of me and my work.

CONTENTS

ACKNOWLEDGMENTS

I thank my entire family for the balanced, loving environment that established my foundation here on Mother Earth. Their consistent, loving support allows me the space to create, share, and teach. Thank you to Antoinette Lembo, Alphonse Lembo, Mary Ann Garofala, and Nick Lembo.

I wish to make a special note of gratitude to Vic Affatagato, who introduced me to *The Magic of Believing* by Claude Bristol. When I was just a little girl, Vic taught me that our thoughts create our reality.

Thank you to The Crystal Garden and my always fabulous staff. I wish to thank Terri Bridgwater, Monika Feigl, Pam Elliott, Marguerite Barringer, and Dawn Seiler for the years of editing and proofreading my articles, which are the foundation for this book, as well as for the support and encouragement they provided.

I am also grateful to Doreen Virtue, Josie RavenWing, Karen McCoy, Robin Rose, Hernan Quinones, Michael Mirdad, Caroline Sutherland, James Wanless, Todd Michael, and Sondra Ray for their insights, wisdom, and support over the years.

A special thank-you goes to my dear friend Melissa Applegate for helping with the editing of this book—but more important, for her genuine, consistent friendship. Thank you also to Mary Martin and Carol Rosenberg for their editorial support and knowledge, as well as to Kim Weiss, whose experience in the publishing business contributed greatly to bringing this book into the world.

In addition, I want to thank the seminar coordinators of bookstores, the Coalition of Visionary Resources (COVR), conventions, conferences, and expos that have invited me to speak, perform, teach, or facilitate. I would like to make a special note of gratitude to Susie Hare of the International New Age Trade Show (INATS) for her belief in me by inviting me to emcee banquets and events for INATS East and West.

Gratitude also goes to Kathy McGee, editor in chief of *New Age Retailer Magazine*, who has provided consistent support and vision. Thank you to Leah Lou Patton of Palm Beach County's *Natural Awakenings* magazine for her continuous marketing support. I express gratitude to *Aura Magazine* and *Enlightened Practice Yoga Journal* for publishing my articles over the years. Thank you to Andrea de Michaelis of *Horizons* magazine for sharing my articles alongside articles by well-established and respected authors.

With love and gratitude to Ted Andrews, who opened the door to Llewellyn Worldwide to usher me into the world of publishing. His introduction and endorsement facilitated the birth of this book, along with the foresight of Bill Krause, who recognized my work with crystals and gemstones. Thank you to Carrie Obry, whose extreme patience and editorial knowledge brought this book into reality.

Last but not least, I am grateful to my sweetheart, Vincent Velardez. His love, support, and consistent reminders to stay focused helped me create the reality of this book.

INTRODUCTION

You can transform your life if you choose. You can be healthier, happier, and more content. Ask yourself, do you feel spiritually fulfilled? Are you living at your optimum emotional level? Do you feel energetic, enthusiastic, and happy to face each day? Inner peace and higher awareness are available through many different paths, one of which is self-awareness, a powerful yet simple method for uniting body, mind, and spirit. Are you truly aware of what you think and feel daily? Have you noticed all the inner chatter repetitively circling through your mind? Self-awareness and being truly conscious of your thoughts, feelings, and actions can shift your reality and lead you to a deeply positive life experience. I truly believe a joyful life is yours for the taking.

But where should you begin? That's what I'm here to help you decide. A plethora of tools are available to you to help escalate your self-awareness and transform your life, ranging from the use of crystals, gemstones, color, sound, and scent to your intention (your active thoughts and desires), all of which can be used singularly or in combination. The ancient spiritual tools presented in this book—many of which are derived from Toltec wisdom as well as from the teachings of the Mayans, Incans, and Native Americans—can be used on a daily basis to effect and maintain positive change in one's life. Whatever tools you choose, what you are doing is working with the energy of life, using these techniques to harness the power of vibration.

Whatever the source, all energy vibrates outward and directly affects the additional vibrations it comes into contact with. You are one more element in this always-vibrating universe. Your emotions, thoughts, and life situations release energy and, therefore, vibrations. With relative ease, you can become aware of the energy you are releasing into the world and achieve vibrational harmony and positive change. In much the same way, this book will also help bring you into harmony with your chakra system. Whether this is your first or your fifth book about working with your chakras, I provide an avenue for a deeper understanding of the chakra system as it relates to vibrational harmony, or overall well-being. The chakras, vibrant energy centers located in and around your body, affect you on all levels—mentally, emotionally, spiritually, and physically. Your entire life experience—beliefs, long-held feelings, and the foundation established early on by family and friends—is crucial information stored within your chakras. As we delve into the characteristics and issues related to each of the seven main chakras, you'll be able to bring your life into better alignment just through becoming aware of what's stored within your consciousness—and it's your consciousness that creates your reality.

In this book, color, crystals, and the chakras are the main spiritual tools we'll use to restore balance to your life. I'll help you understand colors and how they affect you, then build upon that knowledge by incorporating each of the chakras, all of which are associated with a color. Once you have a handle on this, you'll be able to use crystals based on their color for the purposes of focusing intent and creating positive affirmations.

I chose the tools in this book because the teachings and wisdom rang true for me. They were familiar and returned me to my center. As I put them into practice in my life, I improved myself on many levels. My method of practice is to constantly observe myself. I look at myself as an objective observer, as best as I can, to watch my actions and reactions. Through the simple tool of self-observation with love and without judgment, I've transformed many challenges that have arisen. You, too, can incorporate the many principles and teachings into your own life and find more peace, compassion, and love for yourself and others.

ROCKS, CRYSTALS, AND STONES

Crystals can be used to recalibrate your personal energy to vibrate at a rate more conducive to communication with your higher wisdom and divine consciousness. Plus, they're simply beautiful.

The words crystals, gemstones, minerals, rocks, and stones are used interchangeably throughout this book. Crystals, such as quartz and other precious and semi-precious stones, each vibrate at a specific rate. Quartz crystals, including amethyst, citrine, rose quartz, and smoky quartz, are the most common stones used in metaphysical practices; however, this book covers a vast array of gemstones as they relate to the chakras and various emotions, thoughts, and situations, which also vibrate at different frequencies. Positive affirmations used with each stone can help replace negative thoughts and vibrations and assist in bringing about transformation and change.

You can buy gemstones at metaphysical or New Age bookstores around the country. Rocks can be found at old-fashioned rock shops or gem shows, and you can also mine them yourself. I have visited the quartz capital of the United States, the Ouachita (pronounced "wash-it-taw") mountain region in Arkansas, which is noted for its fine quality quartz crystal. It's fun to drive up to the mine site and find clear quartz points sparkling at you, embedded in the clay parking lot.

Gemstones are located in veins in mountains. A rock quarry or a mine site is a place that has been blasted out the side of a mountain to get to the treasures within. The portion open to the public is an area where the miners have dumped excess clay removed from the quarry with huge landmoving equipment to make room to get to more good rocks. I have spent many hours scrambling around big piles of red clay that are chock-full of crystals. It's so much fun to dig through the clay to get to the shiny crystals.

Of course, crystals and gems can be found all around the world. Mount Ida in Montgomery County, Arkansas, has been a center for extensive mining for over a hundred years. Other minerals found in the area are wavellite, veriscite, and sphalerite; also traces of gold, silver, and copper have been found. Brazil is a great mining source of large deposits of quartz crystals. The largest crystal ever found was mined in Brazil. Some of the most beautiful gemstones I've ever seen have come from Minas Gerais, Brazil. *Minas Gerais* means "general mines" in Portuguese. Uraguay has the deepest, richest amethyst. There are also mines throughout France, Mexico, and other places in the world.

The price range of crystals is wide and varied. The most affordable gemstones are tumbled stones, which are usually $1–$5 each. Most metaphysical or New Age stores have a section with bowls or containers filled with a rainbow of tumbled stones. The price of unique specimens and larger pieces of minerals depends on the quality, rarity, and size of the gemstone. There is always a stone for you at the right price. I recommend starting a collection of tumbled stones because you can easily accumulate a rainbow collection of stones at a good price to use as recommended within this book.

SENSATIONAL TOOLS

The power of scent in one's life is quite valuable in spiritual practice as well as day-to-day living. Although scents are not visible to the naked eye, they are a focal part of our lives and provide information for our basic needs, including survival, nutrition, and mating. Essential oils and aromatic herbs can provide physical, mental, emotional, and spiritual benefits that bring the chakras into further alignment. Another spiritual tool discussed in this book is sound. The vibrations produced by chanting, playing soothing music, or drumming can positively impact the vibrational energy of the chakras.

Most importantly, perhaps, the foundation for the teachings in this book is *intention*. Everything created is created through intention. We create our lives with our thoughts, actions, words, and deeds. Our thoughts vibrate out and return back to us in the form of our personal reality. For example, if you think about and visualize getting up for a drink of water, in short order you will be drinking a glass of water. Apply this same example to larger life issues. What you place your attention on creating comes to you through repetitive thoughts and visualization, just as you visualized drinking a glass of water. Although this may sound simple on the surface, your thoughts and intentions can be amplified and actualized through the use of the spiritual tools discussed in this book. Keep in mind that it is not the tool itself that is bringing about the changes; rather, it is your intention behind using the particular tool that effects change.

Much like a program running in the background of a computer, some of your feelings and memories are stored far below the surface of your awareness. Most people aren't really conscious of what they are thinking time and again throughout the day, littering their reality with thoughts that are often negative, self-effacing, repetitive, and redundant. Through following the practices discussed in this book, this "program" or the feelings or memories creating your reality should become evident. Once you are aware of what you are feeling and thinking, you can make a decision to delete anything that doesn't serve you well, just like you would delete an unnecessary program running in the background of your computer.

The key is to use your intention combined with the tools provided in this book. With a little bit of know-how, anyone can change intention into reality. The principles I've gathered here have been practiced by many cultures for thousands of years. Since ancient time, the indigenous people of Europe and Asia have practiced the art of using herbs, crystals, gemstones, aromatherapy, sacred water (water infused with positive intentions, such as holy water), and sound to heal the body, mind, and spirit. Western civilization is only now beginning to catch up to its Eastern neighbors. The interest in and practice of living in harmony with all life grows exponentially each year in the West. Even medical doctors and traditional psychotherapists incorporate metaphysical and spiritual tools into their practices to assist clients who have been looking for ways to improve their lives and health.

The Journey to Chakra Awareness

As I hinted at before, as you begin your journey through this book, it's key to keep in mind that *everything* is energy. Even our physical bodies are surrounded by auras and an invisible etheric field, which we will discuss in more detail later. Energy flows inside our bodies through a network of meridians, or pathways. Healing through Chinese medicine and acupuncture, which have been used for thousands of years, is based upon the balanced flow of energy through these meridians (which are also directly related to the chakra system).

Chapter 1 discusses the spiritual tools at length and how to prepare to use them effectively in your spiritual practice. Chapters 2 through 8 provide the basics of each chakra, including the primary and complementary colors, balancing stones, location, musical note, helpful essential oils, keywords, and the physical body parts directly affected by or associated with each chakra. As you read, you will gain deeper insights about yourself and others. Do the exercises provided in each chapter and take note of profound realizations. Chapter 9 offers information about the quartz family of crystals. This chapter covers clearing stones, recognizing different faces and types of quartz formations and how to work with them to gain a stronger spiritual connection. The gemstone chart in the appendix provides all the necessary information for choosing and using gemstones and crystals for healing and/or manifestation. The appendix also includes a reference chart for sound, color, stones, and oils associated with each chakra; a chakra evaluation table; and an A to Z gemstone guide to conditions and intentions, which sums up all the information found throughout the book.

MY BACKGROUND

This book has evolved from twenty-one years of personal observation, research, and teaching spiritual development and healing classes at The Crystal Garden, a spiritual store and center I established in Florida in 1988. I have also had the fortune of hosting some of the most amazing teachers and medicine men and women from all over the world, and leading trips to sacred sites around the world, all of which furthered my understanding of the spiritual practices and teachings of a wide variety of wise men and women from various cultures.

My workshops become a spiritual portal for participants and practitioners to acquire the wisdom necessary to make changes through conscious awareness. I've been fortunate to witness countless cases of positive transformation as a result of these workshops. Some participants have made career changes, chose, a different path in their relationship, or moved their residence. Moreover, this understanding fosters compassion for themselves and for those with whom they interact, thus improving their personal and professional relationships—and, ultimately, their relationships with all beings. In addition to improved relationships with oneself and others, this gentle approach to self-improvement has helped many people break addictions, take appropriate action toward a goal, make important career choices, and so on.

For example, Joseph is an extremely intelligent man who works in the corporate world. He has hundreds of employees who are caregivers of property and people. He is highly respected, well liked, and makes a good income at his career. After taking one of my crystal healer courses, Joseph stepped onto a new path. He is currently in massage school as he works full-time. He recognized his talent as a spiritual healer, teacher, and counselor and acknowledged that it's time to shift his life more fully into his divine purpose. He has made a conscious decision to leave corporate America to follow his dream of a spiritual career, which fulfills a lifelong desire.

Another participant from the course, Irene, was working full-time in what she considered a mediocre job. She was married to a man whom she cared for, yet she knew he wasn't the ultimate soulmate and lover she was meant to be with for this lifetime. The week after taking the course, she left her job and moved out of her relationship and home. She took these actions consciously. Irene realized freedom and relief and is now pursuing her dream of being an artist and feng shui practitioner. She was able to leave her relationship with love, grace, and good communication.

I have witnessed the transformation of many lives because of understanding the chakras and using color, crystals, and aromatherapy to make conscious changes. You can do the same. You can use this book as the tool to re-create your life the way you intend it to be. What do you want to transform? How do you want your life to be?

one

Spiritual Tools for Cleansing and Healing

*Y*ou create your life much like a gardener creates a garden. The plot is cleared of weeds and debris, the soil is turned and fertilized, and the appropriate seeds are chosen based on the specific things you would like to grow. Once the seeds are planted, you water and nurture them. As time goes on, you prune away unwanted growth and continue to fertilize, water, and nurture the garden. Through this attention and focus, you create a beautiful, natural sanctuary filled with color, scent, and peace.

Much like a garden, our bodies and our consciousness need to be carefully tended to as we grow and ultimately blossom throughout life. The first step is preparing the "soil." In much the same way a gardener prepares a plot by removing debris, one's physical and spiritual space must be cleared of negative energy to allow room for the positive vibrations that bring the chakras and one's overall life into alignment.

As your personal happiness and harmony is the ultimate goal of this book, this chapter begins with a discussion of the chakras and how to perform a chakra alignment. Next, it introduces the spiritual tools that can be used to clear one's physical and spiritual space to ultimately enjoy the physical, mental, emotional, and spiritual well-being that comes from being in balance, bringing your life into full bloom.

SPINNING WHEELS OF LIGHT

Written knowledge of the chakra system, which is based on yoga philosophy, goes as far back as 2000 BCE and can be found in ancient spiritual texts such as the Vedas (2000–600 BCE) and the Yoga Sutras of Patanjali (200 CE). The word *chakra* is a Sanskrit word for "wheel" or "vortex." The seven main chakras or energy centers that make up your body begin at the base of the spine with the root chakra and end at the head with the crown chakra—and all of them are energetically connected. When one or more of your chakras becomes blocked or out of alignment, it affects your mental state or your emotional balance. It can also affect you spiritually. Eventually, a blockage presents itself on the physical level with disease or some health condition that seems to show up out of nowhere.

You may have heard this before, but it bears repeating: You are a spiritual being living in a physical, human body. The physical body you wake up in each morning and put to bed every night, the one that gives you aches and pains or makes you feel elated for finishing a five-mile run, is often the only body we focus on. Just as important to your well-being are your other three bodies: mental, emotional, and spiritual. These bodies comprise your thoughts (mental body), your feelings (emotional body), and your connection with spirit (spiritual body). Even though you can't see your thoughts, feelings, or your spirit, you know they exist—you know how low you feel when someone hurts your feelings.

The landscape of the seven main chakras helps you understand where all four of your bodies are located. The following figure

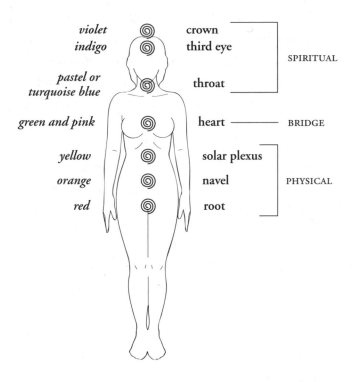

shows the seven chakras and the colors associated with them; they are called the crown, the third eye, the throat, the heart, the solar plexus, the navel, and the root chakras. The lower three chakras are related to the physical part that connects you with the more mundane aspects of living here on planet Earth: food, water, and shelter. The upper three chakras are related to matters of spirit, helping you remember your divine connection to your spiritual nature or your heavenly connection. The heart chakra is the bridge between the upper and lower chakras, bringing heaven to earth and earth to heaven. Imagine the chakras as a divine continuum where physical, emotional, mental, and spiritual needs blend together and emanate from your root to your crown. Keep in mind that the chakras are not flat, static, or one-sided. They are vibrant clusters of energy that radiate in all directions from your body.

Chakras are not stationary or entirely internal. These spinning energy centers encompass the space around the body. For example, the heart center is comprised of a band of energy that extends out from the area where your heart is and wraps around your sides and behind you. Use your imagination and visualize energy radiating around your entire body. These energetic vibrations create your aura, which is thus filled with the colors of the rainbow. The rate at which this abundance of energy vibrates relates directly to the color and sound associated with each of the chakras, which I discuss in the upcoming chapters.

ALIGNING THE CHAKRAS

As we discussed before, everything we think and feel, both positive and negative, is contained within this amazing energy field, whether we are conscious of it or not. When we *are* conscious of how our multidimensional life operates, we are able to clear away negative thoughts and feelings, replace them with positive energy to increase well-being, and bring about balance. In the case of serious illness, balancing the energy field is not a replacement for other methods of treatment. It can, however, be used in conjunction with traditional means of healing as complementary therapy. Use the energetic tools in this book to balance the spiritual, mental, and emotional afflictions that manifest on the physical plane. As you delve into the chapters on the chakras, it will become clear how afflictions in your own life or in the lives of those around you manifest as a result of deeper imbalances within various chakras or energy centers.

Unbalanced chakras can lead to a host of mental, emotional, and spiritual challenges. Uncomfortable physical symptoms or actual disease will present itself as a result of an out-of-balance chakra. For example, unwept tears can result in a cold. Unspoken words can manifest as laryngitis. Unresolved emotions or insecurities often manifest as anger or unexpected, explosive reactions. Unbalanced energy stems from emotional or mental stress, itself the result of someone else's negativity or your own internal negative thoughts and beliefs. As you become aware of the colors and chakras, you will uncover the root cause of life's challenges, illnesses, and/or blockages to your ability to create the life you truly desire.

Chakras can be aligned with relative ease, and the way in which you do it is ultimately up to you, whether you use everyday tools and situations, or create a personal ritual or ceremony to heighten the effect. To start, just thinking the thought "I want to align my chakras" helps create the intention to restore balance. As long as your intention is clear and affirmative, the process will be effective and beneficial. You can carry a gemstone in your pocket to represent the color of the chakra you wish to bring in balance and focus your intention on rebalancing an aspect of yourself related to the chakra. At the same time, focus on your intention on what you would like to accomplish.

How do you establish intention? What is intention? Intention is simply a course of action you've designated as an objective or goal. To establish intention, you decide you are going to do something. You do this every day, all day long. For example, if you intend to get up from your chair and go into another room, it is your intention to do so that gets you out of the chair. Your ability to imagine yourself getting up and walking into the other room creates the action; once you imagine it, you do it. Become more conscious of your intentions. Combine your intentions with specifically colored gemstones as they relate to the chakra or energy center you are intending to rebalance.

You can also carry a number of stones with accompanying affirmations either in your memory or written on a piece of paper. Infuse the stones or the paper with an essential oil that complements the chakra or chakras you are intent on balancing. Strategically place gemstones throughout your home, car, and office to remind you of your intention each time you see them. Place a stone in a pillowcase, on a kitchen windowsill, or on your bathroom counter. When you see it, it will bring to mind the intention you established to restore balance in all aspects of your life. Use chapters 2 through 8 as a guide for choosing issues on which to focus, gemstones and essential oils you can use, and positive affirmations to keep in mind.

To add a ceremonial flair to your chakra alignment, set up a private space by arranging a collection of thoughtfully chosen gemstones. Light complementary-colored candles and infuse the space with essential oils. Ambient music adds a nice touch. Recline, anoint yourself with the essential oil, and place the gemstones on and around your chakras while focusing your intention on balance and alignment. Relax, breathe deeply, and enjoy the positive energy.

When I perform a crystal alignment—the laying on of stones with the intention of clearing and balancing the chakras—for my clients at The Crystal Garden, I sit with them and discover why they are exploring this avenue of complementary energy work. We discuss the various challenges they are experiencing spiritually, physically, mentally, and emotionally. I determine which stones are most beneficial for bringing their body, mind, and spirit into balance and place the chosen stones on and around my client while describing the objective for each stone. The client participates in the experience by using conscious intention, which amplifies the effect.

Other spiritual tools, such as guided imagery and meditation, regression therapy, and inner-child work, can be incorporated into the session based on the client's specific needs. Guided imagery dovetails perfectly with a crystal alignment. As the stones are placed on the body, the facilitator describes the color of the stone and how the stone will be beneficial, and creates an image of the potential positive change that will take occur using the spoken word.

I also facilitate regression therapy as part of a crystal alignment. Regression therapy brings you to a place in your past—whether it is in this lifetime (usually ages two to ten) or into a past life. The realizations from the experience heal current life situations. One client, Rhonda, had a pattern of repeating the same relationship with men over and over again. The partners and time changed, but the relationship patterns were exactly the same. In her regression, Rhonda was brought to an incident around age nine when her father had called her fat. She was very hurt by this. While most prepubescent girls are a bit chubby, she didn't know it at the time, and the memory was stored in her consciousness. This memory led to the time in her life when her mother divorced her father. Her father was devastated, and it was around this same time he became distant. He never healed from the breakup, and placed her in the middle of his distress, creating for her a model of relationships with men; the message was that relationships could only be distant or in constant turmoil. Since the regression, Rhonda has gone on to remove that negative pattern and is working toward creating a conscious, loving relationship with a man who is fully available to participate.

During a crystal alignment, I am simply facilitating the process for a client, not causing it. The *client* is the one doing all the work—he or she is remembering, breathing, healing, releasing, and realigning. Making clients active participants in their realignments empowers them to be in control. Their participation helps them claim their own healing process and provides a longer-lasting effect.

Practicing Self-Observation

Are we generally a culture that lacks self-awareness? Self-observation is one of the best means to achieve self-knowledge—that is, the knowledge of one's own philosophies and beliefs. Most philosophies and beliefs are established from birth to age ten and become part of our subconscious. Through the practice of self-observation, we can uncover these unconscious beliefs and determine if those beliefs are in alignment with our personal truth.

Self-observation is the intentional act of observing one's own behaviors, reactions, and actions as an interested, *objective* observer—that is, without judgment. Once the observation is made, a shift generally occurs without much action. The observation is often accompanied by a realization that one's beliefs and thought-forms (manifestations of mental energy) were imposed or established by others; a conscious decision can be made to discard what is no longer appropriate and retain that which has a positive influence.

Through self-observation, one's level of self-importance is also revealed. Self-importance removes one's ability to stay focused on love, kindness, and tolerance. In order to become a better person, the shift of awareness from self-importance to love actualizes inner peace, health, and well-being. Once achieved individually, this self-actualization can be transmitted to others by example. Inner peace brings awareness, awareness brings love, and love brings inner peace.

Many of the enlightened masters lived human lives on this planet with a focus on love. Throughout time, masters like Buddha, Christ, Sai Baba, Babaji, Mother Teresa, and others focused their teachings and attention on love, kindness, compassion, tolerance, and self-knowledge or self-awareness. Throughout this book you will find the terms *Christ consciousness* and *Buddha consciousness*. These terms are not being used in a religious sense, but are spiritual terms that synoptically refer to the human ability to transform and heal while living within the consciousness of love and tolerance, thereby achieving inner peace.

To begin a simple practice of self-observation, start now as you read this book. Observe how you hold the book. Become aware of your hands holding the book. How are you sitting? What are you sitting on, what is it made of, and where did the materials come from? Are you eating or drinking while you read? Do you smell a scent in the air? Is there sufficient lighting as you read? Through these basic observations, you will begin a journey toward conscious awareness of yourself and your surroundings, thereby heightening your perceptions of self and the space around you. These observations are a small stepping stone to a larger sense of self-awareness, including an awareness of your thoughts, where they are coming from, what provoked them, and how to transition yourself out of unhealthy or challenging situations, all of which will be discussed later.

CLEARING NEGATIVE ENERGY

Toxins (negative energy or particles of any kind) can clutter our physical bodies and physical spaces as well as our emotions, thoughts, and energy fields. To create the reality we want, we must begin by clearing away accumulated toxins, such as unhealthy belief systems, outdated thought-forms, and negative vibrations. For example, when you've had a serious argument with someone, you've probably noticed that the stress and discord are so palpable, the air feels almost solid enough to cut with a knife. While this initial feeling may dissipate, residual emotional energy that accompanied those harsh words remains in the space, accumulating with each upsetting occurrence afterwards. Such accumulation is responsible for why you feel good in some places, such as certain stores, workplaces, or friends' homes, while in others, you feel like bolting for the door. The vibrations of all the feelings, actions, words, thoughts, and emotions that occur within a space literally hang in the air and the physical surroundings. These vibrations can be cleared to make way for positively charged energy.

The simplest technique to clear space is through intention, breath, and focus. Simply breathe in through your nose and retain your breath. On the held breath, form the intention to clear the space. Then breathe out forcefully, with the intention of transforming and transmuting anything not in alignment with your highest good or the highest good of all concerned. Immediately repeat the process. This time, make it your intention to refill the space with love, light, and well-being. The formation of your intention, combined with the forceful "out" breath, is the action that actualizes the clearing. (Incidentally, this technique also works for clearing crystals of any accumulated negative energy; see chapter 9.)

Other methods for clearing away negative energy involve the use of specific spiritual tools, including herbs, sound, and crystals, discussed below.

Smudging Herbs

Smudging is the age-old practice of burning herbs, incense, or resins to clear negative vibrations and replace them with goodness and love. It is a perfect accompaniment to prayer and for sending out blessings, as well as inviting and invoking your angels or spirit guides to help you. Focus your intention and imagine that your prayers and intent are traveling within the smoke as it rises and swirls around you and your space.

Burning herbs and/or incense and resins activates the innate qualities stored within the plant's consciousness that are intended to clear out negativity or to usher in sweetness. Combined with intention, smudging is an effective solution for removing stale thoughts, bad vibes from arguments and/or strong disagreements, or energy remaining in the atmosphere after a depression or illness.

Be sure to replace bad vibes with good vibes right away. You can walk into a place—a home, a retail establishment, a restaurant, or anywhere—and pick up the vibes immediately. The same is true when you first meet a person. You either get a good feeling or one that isn't so good. These vibes are stored in the aura or energy field of a person, place, or thing.

Not only does smudging clear away negativity, it also brings forth positive vibrations and energy. For example, the resins frankincense and myrrh were a blend various religious societies used to call forth high-level spiritual energy. The blend is still commonly used today in nondenominational spiritual circles. Other cultures use different blends of herbs, resins, and flowers. After reading this section you may be inspired to make your own blend to invoke ascended masters, angels, spirit guides, Great Spirit, or the Holy Spirit.

Smudging herbs can be purchased in loose or prepackaged forms, but the most popular is sage, usually sold in a prepackaged bundle called a smudge stick. A smudging blend is a combination of herbs and/or resins intended to be burned together. When found in a bundle, you simply light the end of the smudge stick, blow out the flame, and allow the smoldering smoke to clear away negativity using your intention. To catch any burning pieces that fall off the smudge stick, hold a fireproof dish or a beautiful abalone shell beneath it as you walk around.

You can also burn the herbs and resins by placing them on charcoal. Be sure to obtain charcoal used for this specific purpose. Barbecue charcoal will not work, and is not effective or safe to burn indoors. When preparing to burn herbs and/or resins this way, light one section of the charcoal; place it in an abalone shell, censer, or other fireproof dish; and allow the whole piece of charcoal to fully ignite. Censers are often used to burn incense like frankincense and myrrh, which are hardened resins that form solid "tears" that become liquefied and smolder when burned on charcoal. Once the charcoal is well lit, fill the center of it with your chosen smudge blend.

To clear a room of negativity or unwanted energy, carry the burning herbs in the abalone shell to the corners of the room, and using the smoke and your intention, clear the thought-forms out of all the nooks and crannies. Use feathers or a smudge fan made of feathers to waft the smudging blend into the space to move the energy. Just like dust, energy and thought-forms accumulate in the corners of a room more so than in the center. Be sure to send the smoldering smoke toward the windowsills and under tables. Open cabinet doors and closets and smudge away the accumulated energy. Fan the smoke with your intention to clear under shelves and behind furniture. Also imagine the space you are clearing is refilling immediately with love and blessings.

This particular ritual of lighting and burning herbs holds the vibration of all four elements: Fire (the burning), Earth (the herbs), Water (the shell), and Air (as observed in the rising smoke). All four elements work together to clear and cleanse. The elements are the foundation of all life on this planet and are the essential parts of all nature, the fundamental constituents of anything that exists. Invoking the energy of the four elements in a ritual provides the core components of clearing, creating a desired result. This ritual is the foundation of the classical elements in many indigenous cultures, like those used by Native Americans, the Maya and Inca, and Tibetan Buddhists.

The use of herbs as a tool for clearing and blessing space is founded on the core devic energies inherent in all plant life. Devic forces are elemental energies or spirits of the plant which are responsible for holding the blueprint for the plant. The blueprint holds the design for which the plant will be used. It records the color of the leaves, the height, the chemical components, any flowering, and the innate knowledge of whether the main part of the plant is above or below ground, and much more.

Every plant has a purpose. The chemical components are activated when steeped, burned, or extracted. For example, using an herb like sage to clear away negativity can be likened to tile cleaner clearing away grime in a bathtub. Similarly, resins, which are aromatic dried tree or plant sap, are used for clearing and blessings alike. These resins will be described throughout this chapter.

The following herbs and resins can be used for smudging to clear your sacred space:

Amber is tree sap resin used much like copal (see below). It is helpful for maintaining a sacred space and setting healthy boundaries with others. This resin keeps energy-suckers at bay. Burn this resin in your home to keep away people who show up uninvited, overstay their welcome, or continuously borrow your stuff instead of buying their own.

Cedar comes from the evergreen tree found in the United States, Morocco, Algeria, and China. Cedar is a purifier and calls forth good energy. Use cedar to invoke protection. Cedar is a good herb to use when praying. Watch the smoke rise and have faith in your request being received by God, the Great Spirit, or the angelic realm. Cedar is used by some for bringing in the vibration of Christ consciousness and protection.

Copal is an aromatic resin, dried sap, or gum that comes from the ceiba tree found in Mexico, South America, and West Africa. It was used in Mesoamerican cultures as incense offered to the gods. Burn this resin over charcoal to remove negativity. It can also be used for prayers, ceremonies, blessings, and clearings to bring in positive spiritual energy.

Dragon's blood comes from the resin of a tree native to the Canary Islands and Morocco, as well as from a rattan palm found on Indonesian islands. Just as the name implies, it is a dark-red resin that hardens much like tears of frankincense, myrrh, and copal. The droplets or the dried resin are rolled into balls before they are sold. To use it, drop the dragon's blood resin over ignited charcoal. It can be incorporated into candles, lotions, soaps, and stick incense. Dragon's blood also comes in an oil form and helps with psychic protection. This resin can also protect you from less harmful yet still annoying challenges, especially when you are in large groups of people, such as at a fair, airport, or convention.

Frankincense is an aromatic resin derived from trees in Somalia, Ethiopia, and Saudi Arabia, which should be burned over charcoal, as described earlier. It is also available as stick and cone incense. It instills a spiritual energy and raises the vibration of the area in which it is being used. Frankincense clears away what is no longer for the highest good and replaces lower energy with its naturally high vibrations. This scent also brings forth the vibrations of love, compassion, and kindness in alignment with Christ/ Buddha consciousness.

Lavender is grown primarily in France and England, and can also be found in China, Bulgaria, and Russia. Production of lavender in the United States has increased, and both Oregon and Washington are producing some fine essential oils as well. It is useful to add lavender to a blend of dried herbs to help bring in positive energy. Doing this replaces the negative energy with love and well-being. Lavender's sweetness instills positive energy in the same moment that the negative is booted out. Replace that which is removed with something positive to keep the old pattern away.

Myrrh is a reddish-brown aromatic resin, or dried sap, from a thorny, short, sturdy tree found in Somalia, Ethiopia, Sudan, and southern Arabia. It is available in incense form or as a resin for burning over charcoal. Myrrh is a fixative gum, meaning that when it is combined with other resins or oils, it strengthens their vibrations.

Osha root, also known as **lovage,** is a Native American herb of the parsley family, sometimes referred to as bear root. It can be found in the high mountains of the Southwest, as well as in the Pacific Northwest, including British Columbia. Burn osha root or carry a piece in your pocket to ward off negativity. The root is the most potent part and is used for many ailments.

Palo Santo is a tree native to South American countries like Peru and Ecuador. It is a sacred wood whose name means "holy wood." The Inca have used it for centuries as a spiritual remedy for purifying and cleansing. Light the stick of wood and visualize the removal of negative thought-forms as the smoke arises. Use it to clear away "bad spirits." Palo Santo reestablishes balance and peace within the environment and is often used in meditation practices. I prefer to burn Palo Santo in its stick form separately from my smudge blend because it has such a calming, soothing scent filled with powerful energy. I've also used Palo Santo oil as one of the ingredients of my smokeless liquid smudge concoction, described on page 16, which provides a smokeless alternative to smudging.

Rue, ruda, or **stinkweed,** a hardy evergreen plant, is a native of southern Europe. This herb breaks the vibration of spells, curses, and hexes. Remember, however, that it is the power of your thoughts that create your reality. Only by giving credence to curses and hexes do they have any power. If it is your belief system that spells, curses, and/or hexes have power, you can use this herb to keep away jealousy, covetous eyes, or negative thoughts directed towards you. Although you can use rue soap for washing your hands or rue water for washing the floor, do not put it in your bathwater. CAUTION: THIS HERB IS TOXIC. AVOID ALL CONTACT DURING PREGNANCY.

Sage is most often found in the high desert of North America. It is the foundation for most smudge blends, as it is the cornerstone herb for clearing out negative energy. Use of this herb alone is very effective in clearing away negative thoughts and vibrations. Sage is available in many varieties, but wide-leaf white sage is the one I prefer and use most often. Another preferred variety is high desert sage, which has very small leaves and more twigs, but any variety will do the job.

Sandalwood is derived from a fragrant wood from an evergreen tree found in India, Indonesia, Hawaii, and New Caledonia. The scent helps you focus your mind during meditation and prayer. Sandalwood instills peace and encourages spirituality. Mala beads, prayer beads used by Buddhists to keep track of mantras they chant, are often made out of sandalwood. The scent of sandalwood is also an aphrodisiac.

Sweetgrass is a long, wild grass found in North American low-lying or wet areas. It has a sweet fragrance and is also known as vanilla grass and buffalo grass. It is typically braided and dried. Many Native American tribes use sweetgrass for purification, smudging, and prayer. It smolders when it burns and provides a sweet scent that is pleasing to most people. It attracts good spirits, and its scent brings in sweet, loving energy. Burn this herb alone to amplify its positive vibration.

Smokeless Alternatives to Smudging

Are you bothered by smoke? Do you prefer a smokeless smudging blend that generates the same results? You can create your own concoctions to spray in the air as an alternative to smoky smudging herbs. Sage, cedar, blue cypress, lemon, lime, sweet marjoram, Florida Water, flower essences, holy water, and sacred site essences can be added to plain water and placed in a spray bottle for spritzing around just as you would use a smudge blend to purify and cleanse. Sacred site essences are the captured vibrational essence of a sacred location. The creations of a sacred site essence is achieved through prayers, meditation, singing, intention, and movement of the life force contained within the ether of the site. For example, Smudge in Spray, which includes a variety of cleansing medical grade essential oils, Florida Water, sacred site essences, and holy water I've collected from around the world, is a smokeless alternative originally developed for my shop.

To make your own concoction, fill a two-ounce spray bottle about three-quarters full with water. Ordinary tap water is just fine; you will shift the water's vibration with your intent. Add 15–30 drops each of your choice of essential oils, along with flower essences and holy water, sacred site essences (if you happen to have any), and your intention.

To place your intention into the blend, stay focused on the reason you're creating the blend from the moment you start gathering the ingredients, especially when filling the bottle with water. Let go of any thoughts not related to the purpose of the clearing blend. Having focused intent during the entire process of creation adds an additional subtle yet powerful force to the mixture.

You can use all of the ingredients listed above or any combination—leaving out some or adding others. The most important ingredient is your intention because when all is said and done, your intention creates reality. Fill your mind with thoughts of love and well-being. In fact, you can repeat the words "love" and "well-being" as a mantra during the entire creation process to maintain focused intent.

Shake the bottle well before each use, as the oil and water will separate. You can also top off the blend with Florida Water. Florida Water is a type of cologne produced by the Lanman & Kemp-Barclay Company available at bodegas, some grocery stores, and your local metaphysical store. This cologne has been around since 1808, and has a citrusy base along with clove, lavender, and other cleansing, refreshing scents.

To clear yourself, you can place some Florida Water on your hand and put it on the back of your neck. To clear a room, spray it as you would a room deodorizer. Incidentally, at The Crystal Garden, we regularly spray Florida Water to clear the energy after dealing with a challenging situation, and we spray it in the classrooms and healing room after each event. I like to use it in between clients in the room. Florida Water is also excellent for use in a room where someone is or has been ill to refresh the space, clear away the negative thoughts and feelings that arise during illness, and banish sickroom odors.

Florida Water is used for headaches due to excitement or nervousness, and it usually relieves both headaches and underlying stress. I've put it on insect bites to soothe irritation. It is unobtrusive and reminiscent of a flower garden; therefore, most people like the scent. Using Florida Water is a pleasant and easy way to clear away negative vibrations without burning herbs.

Have fun creating your own blends using oils, waters, or essences to clear away any negativity. Perhaps you have a favorite scent from childhood or a family tradition to incorporate into your own personal blend. Let your creative juices flow and remember to put your intention into the bottle!

Sound Clearing

Chanting, hymns, and drumming have been used in spiritual practices for thousands of years. Many acoustic instruments, such as drums, rattles, bells, and bowls, are used in a variety of ways to clear energy and effect change. Healthy organs and other body parts resonate in harmony with the rest of the body, but when a body part is out of harmony, disease exists.

All energy is vibration, and all vibration has sound. Sound shifts the vibration of a space or energy field and has a transformational effect on each of us in our daily lives, as well as in the healing process. For example, when peaceful, calming music is played in a room or space, it promotes serenity and relaxation. Likewise, hearing one's favorite song and singing along, in the car for instance, brings joy. On the other hand, hearing intense booming from another's car at a stoplight can result in agitation. Singing has been used to soothe a baby to sleep, ease the stress of an illness or pain, and bring more joy into one's life. Sound and music create vibrations within and around us.

Many cultures believe chanting—repetitive melodic speaking or singing of a phrase or statement (mantra)—brings focus and peace. Chanting moves energy and assists in connecting spiritually with the Divine. Chanting is a way to tune in to the frequency of love. The chanting of mantras, as practiced by Benedictine and Tibetan monks, creates a path for a dialogue with the Divine. This connection clears energy and transforms the vibrational frequency. The following tools are used for sound clearing.

Chanting is effective for shifting a space's energy. You can even clear a room with sound when it's not occupied. Leaving music playing with purposeful intention in an unoccupied room is sort of like putting a cake in the oven to bake. While the music plays, the energy has time to "bake." By the time the room is occupied again, the energy is ready, clear, and vibrating at a harmonic rate. Try playing the sacred music of a Gregorian or Tibetan chant in your house or office while you're present or while you're away.

In Gregg Braden's books *The Lost Mode of Prayer* and *The God Code*, he describes how ancients have left us descriptions of how to use the invisible force of prayer to balance the body and emotions. Using the sound of the chants and the intentions therein creates a field of energy that places gratitude and blessings vibrationally within the space. The studies show that when a small number of a population find inner peace through the practice of prayer through sound, the peace was reflected in the world around them.

Drums and rattles are excellent tools for clearing energy and shifting one's personal energy. The use of these instruments provides an avenue to release excess or stagnant energy. The banging of the drum and the shaking of a rattle literally shakes up the energy. It can be compared to shaking out or beating a rug to get the dirt out. In this case, beating a drum or shaking a rattle releases what we no longer need or want from the mental, emotional, and spiritual bodies, in addition to our physical bodies. When we drum with intention, another beneficial layer is added.

I have facilitated many drumming circles over the past two decades. At the start of a drumming circle, participants state their intentions: what they want to release and what they want to manifest, or drum in. One of the keys to clearing negative energy is to immediately replace that which was cleared with positive energy. After you've drummed away what you don't want in your life, it is imperative to establish intention and drum in what you do want. To do this, imagine your life as if what you want has already taken place. When you use your imagination while drumming, it sets up a vibration for your desire to manifest.

You can create the space for a drumming circle for yourself and friends. You can make a mesa or altar in the center of the circle with candles, crystals, feathers, statues, or other sacred objects on some special fabric. Use objects you find meaningful. Gather your friends, bring your percussion instruments along, and let the good times roll. Rattle, howl, drum, and get the energy moving! Participating in a drumming circle reduces stress, improves immunity, and creates community.

Crystal singing bowls and Tibetan bells and bowls create vibrational frequencies that resonate with the note associated with each chakra. Made of various metals, Tibetan bells and bowls are used ceremonially and for meditation by Buddhists. The sound calms the nervous systems and enhances brain function. In feng shui, the ancient Chinese art of placement, practitioners use Tibetan bells and bowls to clear the space of unwanted energy.

The sound produced by crystal singing bowls, which are made of quartz, brings positive effects and changes in the body, specifically the autonomic, immune, and endocrine systems. In fact, modern scientists and doctors are integrating this work into medical practice. Mitchell Gaynor, M.D., director of Medical Oncology and Integrative Medicine at the Strang Cancer Prevention Center at Cornell University Medical College, New York, and author of *The Healing Power of Sound: Recovery from Life-Threatening Illness Using Sound, Voice and Music,* uses crystal bowls and Tibetan bowls in his practice with cancer patients. His website and book provide a thorough study of healing with sound with a holistic approach to mind-body healing. Dr. Andrew Weil, M.D., director of Integrative Medicine at the University of Arizona, published a CD with sound therapist Kimba Arem called *Self-Healing with Sound and Music.* He endorses the use of crystal bowls for self-healing.

Everything absorbs and emanates sound, and therefore every atom, molecule, cell, gland, and organ of the human body does so as well. Each crystal singing bowl sounds a specific note, and each note resonates with a specific chakra. The color and sound of the energy centers vibrate those waves we call sound. Each chakra has a note associated with it. For example, the foundational energy center, known as the root chakra, vibrates to the note "C" and its color is red. To clear and retune the root chakra, play a crystal bowl or other music in the key of "C" with the intention to calibrate and realign this energy center.

The playing of the bowls recalibrates and rebalances the chakra system. Purchase a crystal singing bowl CD to use for realignment, or even better, buy some crystal singing bowls. I use a full set of seven bowls, each bowl tuned specifically to each chakra. With intention, I play the bowl using a suede-covered mallet. The tone creates waves that affect the body. The vibrations emanating from the singing bowls create a cocoon or web of well-being.

Crystals and Gemstone Clearing

Crystal grids are the placement of gemstones with intention in specific geometric patterns to produce a web of energy that assists a specific goal. I've created large crystal grids with the help of fellow travelers at sacred sites in Mexico, Peru, Florida, and the Four Corners region of the United States. In these large grids, I used tabular clear quartz crystals. Participants held the intention to activate the grids of light around the planet as we stood around the site in geometric patterns using telepathy. Telepathy, mind-to-mind and heart-to-heart communication, will be explained further in chapter 7.

On a smaller scale, you can create a crystal grid to help you sleep better, improve your business, deflect negativity, or attract better health. Arrange the gemstones in the corners of the room, home, or office. Put them on desks, counters, coffee tables, bookshelves, end tables, mantles, and window sills. Think of the intention—clearing the space of negative energy—while you arrange the stones in positions throughout the living or working environment. Imagine that these stones are creating invisible threads or cords to create geometric patterns that are emanating your intention. The stones will reactivate your intention each time you happen to look at a stone in position, as it brings to mind your original intent to keep your space clear of unwanted negative vibes.

For example, position a selenite log or a bowl of smoky quartz and black tourmaline at the entrance to your home. Insert an amethyst in your pillowcase or hematite in the four corners of your bedroom to create a grid of protection and calm. In the chapters that follow, you will find a plethora of ideas and tools to create a safe and loving environment using gemstones.

SPIRITUAL TOOLS FOR BALANCING THE CHAKRAS AND HEALING THE PHYSICAL, MENTAL, EMOTIONAL, AND SPIRITUAL BODIES

Nature offers healing gifts. These gifts are tools available to align and balance you mentally, physically, spiritually, and emotionally. Plants and minerals provide a plethora of uses. Here you will discover the use of essential oils, flower essences, and crystals for clearing.

Aromatherapy

Aromatherapy is the therapeutic use of pure essential oils derived from plants, flowers, barks, roots, and resins. Essential oils and aromatic plants and herbs have been used for thousands of years. Early records left by ancient Egyptians indicate the use of essential oils for cosmetic purposes and for the preservation of dead bodies for the afterlife. Ancient Greeks and Romans, who bought their oils from Egyptians, used the oils for their healing properties, as well as in their bath houses and temples. Medicinal essential oil formulas have been found inscribed in several ancient temple walls.

Use aromatherapy along with gemstones, guided imagery, and integrative therapies in a chakra-balancing session. The sense of smell and the chemical constituents within the oils have an effect on us physically, mentally, spiritually, and emotionally. Essential oils work on a deep level through the olfactory nerve and the limbic system, which is also known as the reptilian brain, a very primal level of functioning. Through scent and absorption, the chemical components bypass other more conscious avenues of healing, effectuating and activating the healing process.

Oils may be derived from a plant using steam distillation and other extraction techniques. Essential oils are concentrated with hundreds of organic constituents or chemical components, including beneficial phytoestrogens and phytonutrients. Oils can be inhaled by placing a few drops on a handkerchief or within a diffuser. Because of the high level of concentration, all essential oils (with the exception of lavender) need to be diluted in a carrier oil before they can safely be applied to skin. Carrier oils, also called base oils—such as sweet almond, jojoba, sesame, olive, or grapeseed oil—are derived from seeds, vegetables, or nuts, and also have therapeutic properties that nourish the skin. Carrier oils allow the correct amount of essential oil to be spread over a larger portion of the skin without irritation.

When applied topically, the skin absorbs the oil and it enters the bloodstream. Rubbing the oil onto the bottom of one's feet is an effective way of getting the essential oil into one's system. The principal tenet of reflexology is that each body organ corresponds to areas on the bottom of the feet. According to *The Complete Guide to Foot Reflexology* by Barbara and Kevin Kunz, reflexology is the physical act of applying pressure to feet based on a system of zones that represent the image of various organs or parts of the body. For more than 2,000 years, acupuncture physicians have used points on both sides of the feet and the big toes. Even the Cherokee of North Carolina used pressure treatment on the feet for healing. Therefore, the strategic placement of essential oils on the feet can benefit body areas in need.

Try it for yourself. For example, if you are feeling the very start of a cold or a sore throat, place a few drops of eucalyptus oil into a dollop of unscented moisturizing lotion in the palm of your hand. Blend it together and then massage the eucalyptus-scented lotion onto the bottom of the your feet. Be sure to do your research before applying essential oils to your body, however.

Chapters 2 through 9 each include a discussion of the most relevant essential oils to use with each of the chakras or color energy. Whenever you use an essential oil, use it with intention. Visualize and make a conscious intention with your thoughts, words, and actions. Imagine yourself rebalanced and realigned.

Be sure to do your research to determine if there are any precautions you should be aware of before using a certain oil. The chemical components in essential oils can have a significant effect on the body. For example, clary sage, sweet marjoram, and ylang ylang can lower blood pressure, and should therefore be avoided by people with low blood pressure. Some oils are phototoxic, which means they increase the effect of sunlight. Phototoxic oils should never be used on the skin before exposure to the sun. Most citrus oils are phototoxic. The only essential oil that can be used neat (without dilution) is lavender; every other oil must be diluted. To be on the safe side, even a citrus oil in a carrier should be avoided before going out into the sunlight.

Be sure to purchase only those oils that are truly medical grade or therapeutic quality. At my shop, for example, we hand-fill bottles of medical grade essential oils. With our own private-label oils, we are certain our products are therapeutic medical grade and that they may be used on the body, usually with a carrier oil. Medical grade oils do not contain any synthetic or non-natural adulterations. On the other hand, aromatherapy grade oils are sometimes adulterated with natural and non-natural components, and commercial grade oils are distilled or have components added or removed. Therefore, when you shop for essential oils, buy only therapeutic or medical grade oils. If it's not apparent, ask the salesclerk whether the oils are commercial or medical grade. If they aren't medical grade, don't buy them.

Two good resources for learning how to use essential oils for yourself and others are *Essential Aromatherapy: A Pocket Guide to Essential Oils and Aromatherapy* by Susan Worwood and *The Directory of Essential Oils* by Wanda Sellar. (Also see the References section at the back of this book.)

Essences for Healing Mental and Emotional Imbalances

Most of us are familiar with the use of herbs for healing and balancing the subtle and physical bodies. On a vibrational level, the energy of a plant, herb, or tree has balancing properties. The most commonly used flower essences are Bach Flower Essences, which are drawn from the essence of wildflower blooms. There are thirty-eight plant- and flower-based formulas that can help manage life's emotional demands. They are vibrational, not traditional extracts, because the plant or flower's energy is used. To use these essences, I place a drop or two of the remedy I need into a bottle of water, thereby changing its vibrational frequency.

The use of flower essences for healing is known as vibrational medicine. As you know, for good health, well-being, and wholeness, energy must vibrate at a frequency or rate aligned with those positive qualities. Essences, such as Bach Flower Remedies and other flower essences, as well as sacred site essences and sacred water, are used to bring these vibrations into alignment. While essential oils are derived from plants and have actual chemical properties, essences are strictly vibrational and contain no physical components.

In the 1930s, Dr. Edward Bach (1886–1936), a medical doctor and bacteriologist, realized that disease is an end product or a final stage; a physical manifestation of unhappiness, fear, and worry. He developed a system of infusing spring water with wild flowers either by boiling or a sun-steeping method. The vibrational essence of a plant comes from the energy stored within it. From this, he developed thirty-eight flower-based formulas that have the ability to rebalance the spiritual, mental, and emotional bodies. These remedies help shift negative attitudes and feelings. They restore the balance between mind and body by casting out negative emotions, such as, fear, worry, hatred, and indecision, which interfere with the mental and emotional balance. The Bach Flower Remedies allow peace and happiness to return so that the body is free to heal itself.

All the plants in our world have value, and I personally have had very good results working with flower essences. To use Bach Flower Remedies, place drops of the essences needed into drinking water. Drink the water throughout the day combined with the intention of releasing the challenges you are experiencing. It is also beneficial to add a few drops of flower essences into a bathtub, as it is then absorbed on a much greater scale. A few drops in a large tub of warm water changes the qualities of the bathwater.

The essence combined with your intention will amplify the benefits. For example, when I was in the process of becoming a nonsmoker, I employed Bach Flower Remedies for anxiety, anger, and fear of the unknown, and to clear away the unclean feeling of the tobacco in my system. I used Aspen for anxiety and fear of the unknown, Cherry Plum for the fits of rage that came with taking away those cigarettes, and Crab Apple for uncleanliness.

One of the most popular flower essences is Rescue Remedy which is made up of five flower remedies for trauma, stress, anxiety, and shock. This five-flower formula uses Impatiens, Star of Bethlehem, Cherry Plum, Rock Rose, and Clematis. It is recommended for use when you first hear of upsetting news, to balance the shock of an accident or an emergency, for use before an exam or for any other situation in which you can lose mental balance. Over the years of personal experience as well as observations from my customers who buy the Bach Flower Remedies at my store, the effectiveness of these essences has been proven to me over and over again.

The remedies work very well for children who have temper tantrums and/or night terrors. Bach Flower Remedies are safe for children; in fact, Bach Flower Remedies have an alcohol-free Kid's Rescue Remedy. Many people use Rescue Remedy for their dog's fears, such as a fear of thunderstorms or other behavioral problems, by placing a drop in the dog's drinking water as recommended by veterinarians.

Dr. Bach put his remedies into seven categories: fear, uncertainty, insufficient interest in present circumstances, loneliness, oversensitivity to influences and ideas, despondency and despair, and over-care for the welfare of others. You can determine which of the essences you need by reading through each of the descriptions for all thirty-eight remedies. The emotional imbalance that each essence was designed to correct is specifically described, allowing you to identify the best essences for you.

The use of flower essences is a complementary program to a more traditional approach for rebalancing mental and emotional challenges. For example, Cherry Plum balances the need for emotional eating and helps you stay in control when tempted by cravings. Likewise, Crab Apple helps you feel better about your body, while Chestnut Bud aligns you so that you will choose healthier eating options.

The use of flower essences works well with the teachings of Louise Hay, as she shares in her book *Heal Your Body* (Hay House Publishing, 2000). She believes that through the power of your thought-forms, you create your reality and your health (or lack thereof). She healed herself from cancer through the use of positive affirmations and loving herself. Use Louise Hay's positive affirmations combined with Bach's Flower Remedies as a winning combination for energetic self-healing.

Just as flowers, plants, and trees vibrate at a certain rate, the site of a sacred place has a vibrational rate. Sacred sites are places where temples, pyramids, and churches stand. These are places where people pray or have performed ceremonies, or where miracles have taken place. These vibrations can be "captured" in water, thereby creating a sacred site essence. Once captured in the water, the vibration is maintained with one's intent to assist. Sacred site essences can also be holy waters collected from streams or wells where many people make pilgrimages. Holy water and water instilled with intention works well for rebalancing and healing.

The tools necessary to create an essence are amber, cobalt, or green-colored glass bottles with dropper tops; cleared and charged tiny quartz crystals; and clean, purified, or distilled water. You can find the bottles at your local apothecary, aromatherapy, or metaphysical gift store. The tiny quartz crystals can be found at your local rock shop or metaphysical store. You will need to program the crystals, a process described in chapter 9. Fill the bottles with the water and add the programmed clear quartz crystals. Do not cap the bottle until after you have completed prayers, songs, chants, and/or a meditation at the sacred site while holding the intention so that good vibrations are transmitted from the site into the bottle. When you are done, cap the bottle.

You also can make holy water by praying and sending the words into the water with your intention. By speaking into the water and saying words such as "love and gratitude," you can alter the molecular and vibrational structure of the water. Hold your intention to vibrate at the rate of love and gratitude as you instill that intention into the water. Another way to do this is to write the words "love and gratitude" on a piece of paper, face the words toward the water, and intend that vibration into the water.

Masaru Emoto is a renowned Japanese researcher and doctor of alternative medicine. Emoto's research has visually captured the structure of water by taking pictures of ice crystals through high-speed photography. His research documents the direct results of destructive thoughts and thoughts of love and well-being on the formation of water crystals. Emoto showed that words and intention can change the vibrational frequency of the water. As our bodies are made up of approximately 70 percent water, it's clear how words, thoughts, and actions can affect our bodies, minds, and spirits. In *The Hidden Messages in Water* (Beyond Words Publishing, 2004), Emoto reports that "water has a memory and carries within it our thoughts and prayers. As you yourself are water, no matter where you are, your prayers will be carried to the rest of the world."

Crystals and Gemstones for Healing and Balance

Crystals and gemstones are excellent tools that can be used for healing and restoring balance. Crystals should be used in combination with intention, which is key in this practice. Crystals are tools for manifesting. Put your intention into the stone by gazing at it and acknowledging that every time you touch it, look at it, or think of it, it will help you refocus your attention and awareness on your intention, thereby bringing you a step closer to the reality being created.

Of course, the use of crystals/gemstones goes far beyond just wearing the stone as jewelry or carrying the stone around in your pocket, purse, or briefcase, but it is a good way to begin incorporating gemstone use into your daily life. You can even place gemstones in your pillowcase at night, focus on your desired intention, and allow them to work while you sleep. While carrying or focusing on a crystal/gemstone, make it your intention to magnify your goal.

Mother Earth has provided tools to help in all the colors of the rainbow, in every shape imaginable. Each gemstone relates directly to one or more of your chakras as they relate to the color and what balance is needed. In some cases, the complementary color is more effective than the normally designated color assigned to each chakra, as you will learn later in this book. To determine which gemstone you should use, it is best to be aware of the colors associated with each chakra (see the diagram on page 3) as well as the meaning and purpose of each chakra discussed in the chapters to follow. With this foundational knowledge, you can move forward using gemstones in your daily life for balance, health, and well-being.

Each chapter includes a discussion of crystal/gemstones as it relates to a particular chakra and color energy and provides affirmations for use with the crystals. Gemstones such as agate, quartz, tourmaline, calcite, and jasper come in a variety of colors and will therefore appear under more than one color energy or chakra. It's important to note that although the actual minerals hold specific vibrations, the color of the stone is a more significant consideration in conjunction with the area of consciousness being affected.

Although it's beneficial to know each gemstone's quality, simply observing the color can clue you in on its healing and balancing properties. However, once you have covered the material on each chakra and its associated colors in the upcoming chapters, you'll be able to determine which crystals/gemstones to use for specific mental, emotional, and spiritual healing.

Every time you see or touch a stone, you will be reactivating your intention and creating your reality. Let the crystals and gemstones shine their light and add the full spectrum of color to light up your reality with joy, happiness, health, wealth, and laughter.

As you read further, you'll discover a deeper knowledge and understanding of the various colors and shades that fall between those listed on page 3. Each of us is a living, breathing rainbow of sound, color, and vibration.

A Ritual: Honoring the Seven Directions

Using a ritual at the beginning of a new journey, such as learning about rebalancing your chakras, is a good way to invite new experiences and knowledge into your life. Ritual is a wonderful way to realign yourself on all levels, and the act speaks to your soul. Performing a ritual is a sacred and meaningful process by which you can connect with the deeper essence of yourself. Rituals inspire and open the consciousness to bring forth awareness that may have otherwise lain dormant. Create a soul-centered ceremony to align with your practical reality and watch how your perspective on life changes. Rituals create a doorway to higher truth and deeper understanding.

The following ritual invokes the seven directions and can serve as a template or foundation for the opening of any ceremony or prayerful experience. Invite the sacred into your daily life. Feel free to include objects in this ritual or invocation. Sacred objects provide a focal point to help maintain concentration and prevent the mind from wandering. Some objects you may want to include are candles, incense, sage, crystals, an empty bowl, a rattle or a drum, and flowers. As the ritual progresses, allow inspiration to direct how to use the objects, or just let them be on a table or altar before you.

Creating an altar is as simple as setting a cloth in front of you and placing the objects of choice on it. The beginning of a ritual is often called an invocation because you are invoking or inviting specific deities, spirit guides, angels, or elements to be present for the ritual. In the following invocation, I honor the seven directions.

Most often, we view our world as having four directions: north, south, east, and west. The other three directions are above, below, and within. The within direction is the place of the heart, where we are connected with all people and all things. This ritual or invocation establishes a connection to expanded awareness, increasing the dimensionality of existence. It also invites the vibrations of all aspects of life here on earth. This simple prayer is set up as though you and I are sitting together in a circle, about to enter into the subject matter of this book.

For a prayer ceremony, I invoke the energy of all seven directions. Using the sacred smudge or Smudge in Spray, I invite and invoke the energy of the East, South, West, North, Above, Below, and Within.

> *From the east, we invite the intention of clarity of mind to absorb*
> *this body of work.*
> *From the south, we invoke healing and transformation.*
> *From the west, we ask for introspection to go within the self to*
> *know personal truth.*
> *From the north, we request wisdom and knowledge from our*
> *ancestors.*
> *From the sky above, we call upon our guides and angels to inspire*
> *and enlighten*
> *From the earth below, we have gratitude for this life experience*
> *here on the planet.*
> *From within, we realize that we are all one. We are connected.*
> *Hey! Hey!*

This ritual works well with or without burning incense, candles, or herbs. It can be done in a solitary practice to invite and invoke guardians and archangels to shine their presence upon a space or a building. It is also effective for creating sacred site essences in order to invoke the vibration of the site. Amend this ritual to your specific needs.

———

In the chapters that follow, you will walk through the rainbow of colors of the human energy field—the chakras—that hold the blueprint for specific aspects of the subtle and physical body. The subtle body includes your spiritual, mental, and emotional makeup. As you integrate and understand the colors associated with each chakra, you will come to know the specific meanings of the crystals/gemstones and other spiritual tools that complement them.

two

RED ENERGY
AND THE
ROOT CHAKRA

*T*he root chakra is the foundation on which all the other chakras are built. It is the area responsible for basic survival needs like food, water, and shelter. Everything starts with a foundation, and so it is with the human energy system. Your physical entrance into this world was through the root chakras of your mother and father. The first ten years of your life create the foundation from which you act and react for the rest of your life.

The root chakra is located at the base of the spine, at the coccyx. The primary color associated with the root chakra is red, and it also holds the vibration of black, brown, and silvery gray, like the mineral hematite. The root chakra connects you with Mother Earth. What color is soil? Depending on where you live, the soil is typically red, brown, or black.

THE ROOT CHAKRA

Primary Colors: Red, black, brown, silvery gray

Complementary Colors: Blue, green

Stones: Agate, black tourmaline, garnet, hematite, jasper, obsidian, ruby

Other Stones for Balance: Chrysocolla, lapis lazuli, sodalite, turquoise

Location: Coccyx, at the base of the spine

Musical Note: C

Essential Oils: Patchouli, spikenard, vetiver

Keywords: Abundance, earth connection, grounded, focused, kundalini, passion, physical energy, self-motivated, survival needs

Physical Body: Bladder, blood, male reproductive organs, nervous system, spine, testes, vagina

CHARACTERISTICS OF THE ROOT CHAKRA

Just as the roots of a tree determine its life and strength, so, too, are the roots of the self a strong determining factor in personal growth. The physical part of a human being requires a place to live, food to eat, and water to drink. Physical vitality depends upon nutrition and protection from the elements, along with a safe place to sleep and pure water to drink. The ability to stay focused on and achieve tasks is located at this chakra.

The Foundation: Food, Water, and Shelter

Just like any building or physical structure, the human body—the physical body, the emotional body, the mental body, and the spiritual body—needs a good, strong foundation. The root chakra located at the base of the spine is the foundation upon which the rest of the chakra system is built. This center is responsible for fulfilling your basic needs. The root chakra can be compared to the base of the pyramid of Maslow's Hierarchy of Needs or Pyramid of Self-Actualization. At the base of this pyramid are basic survival needs.

Once you have your basic needs met, you are able to move forward and begin balancing the other chakras. Without basics like money, you are less likely to focus on the full development of your upper chakras. You don't have to be rich to be spiritually aligned, but abundance will automatically fall into place when you are. And if you're not, something in your life will occur to shift your awareness into alignment.

In 2004 and 2005, many major hurricanes hit south Florida. Root chakra stability for everyone in the area was threatened. Great shifts in awareness can be achieved during stressful times when basic foundational issues are endangered. All that is comfortable and normal may suddenly be blown away, as if the Big Bad Wolf had rolled into your neighborhood and blown your house down, creating a heightened sense of awareness.

This type of experience actually strengthens your foundation, and life becomes crystal clear. Many people realize it is time to leave a job, end a relationship, or commit more fully to a relationship, and so on. In other words, the threat of life-changing events brings clarity. People stop living complacently, maintaining the status quo, and make necessary changes to live life fully and happily.

Prosperity

Your prosperity consciousness resides in the root chakra. Prosperity consciousness incorporates all the belief systems you have about money. How do you feel about being wealthy? Do you like rich people? Do you feel you deserve to be paid for your work? How did your family deal with money? Do you save money? Can you accept that there is plenty for everyone and everyone can be prosperous? These core foundational beliefs are formed at a very young age.

If you regularly struggle with financial security and you are ready to transform that pattern, then it is time to delve into the core issues in your life and the foundational belief system that you grew up with. It may be that you took vows of poverty in one or more past lives. These vows are usually associated with living a spiritual life, such as being a nun, priest, or monk. If you have any memory or feeling that you lived a monastic life, you probably promised to live a simple life with very few material objects and comforts. If you wish to clear those vows, you can decree that you now release yourself from any vows of poverty you have taken in all directions of time.

The majority of your core beliefs are established in the first ten years of your life. These years are called the formative years for a reason—this is when you store the information that becomes your foundation or your "come from" place for the rest of your life. It may take a wake-up call or a crisis to catapult you into exploring your core beliefs and the events that created those beliefs. Through self-observation and recapitulation of some early events, you can bring about consciousness and awareness. Once you realize what created the beliefs to start with, you can work on healing and re-alignment.

Exercise

RECAPITULATION

The intention of this exercise is to help you remember the belief systems that were imposed upon you as a child. The belief systems helped mold you, but at this moment, you have the opportunity to review these beliefs and decide which ones you want to keep and which ones you are ready to release. Once you clean away what is no longer your truth, you have room to create what you do want in your life. This exercise is part meditation and part writing exercise.

You will need paper (or a journal) and a pen. Turn off phones and other things that could interrupt your meditative process. Sit comfortably in a quiet place with your spine erect. Set the paper and pen somewhere nearby or in your lap. Place all of your awareness on your breath—on the inhalation and the exhalation. Be aware of your hands resting gently in your lap and how your spine supports the structure of your body. Close your eyes and breathe. Observe the expansion of your body when you inhale, and observe the contraction of your body as you exhale. If thoughts arise in your mind, acknowledge them and let them know you will return to them later—right now, you're doing something else. If a thought persists, pick up your pen and write it down to remove it from your consciousness. Keep in mind that a very persistent thought could be a clue for what the exercise is helping you deal with.

As you continue to focus on your breath, let yourself relax. Relax every part of your body, starting with your feet. Take a deep breath and think to yourself: Feet relax. Legs relax. Hips relax. Internal organs relax. Torso relax. Back muscles relax. Shoulders relax. Arms and hands relax. Face and scalp relax.

Put all of your awareness on the center of your forehead and the center of your chest, near your heart. Pick up your pen and write down every place you've ever lived from the moment you were born. If you can, include the address, people, and situations you recall from each residence. Allow yourself to go into a free-reeling journaling session where you allow yourself to write in a stream of consciousness. As you jog your memory, feelings will arise. Allow yourself to feel the feelings and write out what you are experiencing.

This exercise can also be done at your computer if you can keep yourself from being distracted. So if you do better writing or journaling when you type instead of writing longhand, then follow your internal guidance system. The point is to allow an awakening of your awareness to help you find the source of your belief systems. You don't have to change anything, but you may find that the awareness provides the avenue for a shift to take place in a positive way.

It takes motivation, energy, and enthusiasm to create money and abundance. Therefore, your personal health and vital energy are part of your foundational root system. Just like a tree needs sturdy roots to be able to absorb the minerals and nutrients in the soil, the human body needs strong roots as well. The root chakra is responsible for holding the blueprint of your physical vitality.

Vital Energy

The energy, or lack thereof, vibrating at the root chakra regulates your health and your passion for life. Do you have a lot of get-up-and-go or are you always tired? You may need more rest or better nutrition to restore your vital life force. Are you a mover and a shaker, or are you a procrastinator? If you find that you are a procrastinator and aren't able to conjure up the energy to get things done, it's time to light a fire under your root chakra!

Laziness, procrastination, or a lack of motivation could stem from depression or imbalanced nutrition. Both states create an out-of-balance root chakra—it lacks red energy and circulating vitality. Consciously look at your diet and add more (naturally!) red foods. In addition, add red clothes to your life with the intention of activating energy and vitality. Use red stones, wearing them in jewelry or placing a tumbled stone in your pocket. Keep the stones nearby you at home or in your office as a reminder of your intention to make a shift. Make the decision to overcome lethargy, and make it your intention that every day, in every way, you are more and more motivated. Thinking these thoughts will help you achieve your goal.

To activate the root chakra, carry red stones like garnet, ruby, red jasper, and red calcite in your purse, pocket, and/or briefcase; you can also wear them as jewelry. Start a regular exercise regimen, observe what you eat, and make the necessary changes to bring more live food into your diet. Get more sunshine to integrate vital life energy. Notice and look at the color red in your world with conscious intention—that is, projecting the thought as you carry a red stone, wear a red shirt, or look at a red flower—that you are doing so to increase your vital life force and your ability to get things done.

Activating red energy takes focus. Your ability to stay focused and not flitter from one thing to another without accomplishing anything is controlled by your ability to stay grounded and in the present moment.

Focus

If you notice you're a bit spacey, scattered in your thoughts and actions, and just can't focus, grab some hematite, smoky quartz, or black tourmaline and imagine yourself reconnecting with the earth. Visualize roots growing from the soles of your feet into the earth and that they ground you. Imagine you're pulling the earth's consciousness through your whole being. Being grounded, focused, and prosperous is the result of a balanced root chakra.

Wear a hematite ring on your finger or a black tourmaline pendant on your neck, or keep a smoky quartz in your pillowcase while you sleep. Make it your intention that the gemstone within your energy field will amplify your intention to be more grounded, focused, and conscious. When you are focused and conscious, you are safe, because you are alert to any challenges that might arise.

With a steady foundation, you are less likely to become fearful, because your attention is focused and you are aware.

Protection

Safety is another aspect of being strongly rooted. Red and black are colors of protection. Within the kingdom of gemstones, the all-time favorite stone for deflecting negativity is black tourmaline, with hematite coming in a close second. Keeping negative energy away is a logical way to maintain safety. Use red and black stones to protect yourself. Observe lamas, priests, and nuns. The colors of their traditional outfits are most often the root chakra colors. Perhaps these colors were chosen to help them stay focused on prayer and to remain protected as they assist others.

A lack of foundational requirements can sow seeds of fear and anger. Angry people often use anger as a defense mechanism to scare and intimidate others to feel superior. This kind of anger often stems from personal fears caused by a lack of money, resources, or security. Without money, food, water, and shelter will be lacking.

Inflammation

Inflammation in the body appears as a sign that you are feeling somewhat unloved or uncomfortable in some relationship or situation. When out of balance, your chakras can have too much of a color or too little. Too much red energy may overstimulate the root chakra and cause you to become agitated and angry. Alternatively, you may feel passionate and ready to take action.

Inflammation manifests in headaches, swollen joints, arthritis, or any diseases that arise due to an inflamed part of your consciousness. Inflammation shows up in the physical body to get your attention. It alerts you to work on underlying issues, in spite of our human tendency to not want to deal with uncomfortable thoughts, feelings, and situations. Issues that are not addressed in order to avoid confrontation will find other ways to be cleared. Sometimes the first action is to get medicine to mask the symptom, but until true healing takes place on core issues, the physical challenge has a tendency to resurface. Inflamed muscles, like a sprained ankle, for example, will often recur to make you stop, calm down, contemplate, and listen. Pay attention to your thoughts—doing so can help you realize what any underlying anger or fear is really about.

Fear and Anger

The vibrations of fear and anger are stored in the root chakra at the base of the spine. Fear and anger may be counterbalanced by introducing blue and green stones into your energy. Use lapis lazuli, sodalite, malachite, and chrysocolla with cuprite to restore balance.

We've all heard of people being so angry that they "see red." Just the right amount of red energy at this chakra will create a passion for living and the gumption to get up and live life fully. An excess of red stored at the root can result in frustration and anger. Anger itself is actually an emotion expressed out of fear.

Fear is a powerful force. It makes us believe imminent danger is all around us. The danger could be not having enough money, resulting in an inability to pay the rent or the mortgage and subsequently becoming homeless and hungry. These emotions are real, and yet the fear is often false, as the situation (i.e., being actually flat-broke) has not yet occurred. This type of fear breeds anger.

Have you ever noticed how testy you get when you're too hungry? It could be caused by a drop in blood sugar levels, but nevertheless, it still elicits anger. Can you imagine how cranky you would be if you were unable to regularly feed yourself? Prolonged insufficient nutrition creates a physiological imbalance. Similarly, insufficient sleep creates imbalance. Sleep is a core foundational need for maintaining health and vital life force.

Anger is usually destructive, both to us and to those with whom we are angry. Having the calm and rational knowledge to balance fear allows us to deal with challenges in a forthright manner. Turn fear into passion and transform it into a catalyst for change. Transform your fear by giving attention to productive uses of your energy and time. Find an outlet to be of service for a cause. For example, if you identify one of your personal fears as not having enough money due to lack of work, do some volunteer work for a cause you believe in. Invoke assistance from your angels or spirit guides to orchestrate a coincidence so you can meet someone who will be instrumental in obtaining a paying job doing the work you love.

Passion for life and living is stored at the base of the spine. The red vibration creates passionate energy that can be used to fuel your personal motivation to achieve great things. Having passion for a cause, your work, and your loved ones motivates you to keep the flow of life moving for yourself and others.

Kundalini

The passionate vibration of sexual and sensual energy is strongly associated with the human need to survive as a species. The core reproductive functions of the physical body reside at the root and navel chakras. The root chakra is the primary location of male sexual energy. The male sexual organs are located at the first chakra, so male sexual energy is experienced primarily as physical. A woman's sexual organs are located at the second chakra, so female sexual energy is experienced primarily as emotional. Both chakras are associated with sexual energy.

Kundalini—serpent-like, spiritual life force—is coiled at the base of the spine. Based on Hindu and Buddhist philosophies, this spiritual energy lies dormant until it is consciously awakened through yogic practice, and then it is channeled to the head to bring about enlightenment. Using your intention and focus, you can clear and activate the chakras, allowing kundalini to rise. As it rises, it strengthens each chakra on every level, and increases physical vitality. It balances your emotions and your mental outlook. The core of your spiritual foundation is stored at this chakra.

Body Parts Related to the Root Chakra

The physical parts of the body directly related to the root chakra energy system are the blood, nervous system, spine, bladder, and reproductive organs. These body parts maintain survival on a core level of the human body as well as for the human race. In very simplistic terms, the blood, nervous system, and spine are the core vibration that holds us together. The reproductive system is what ensures the human race will continue. The organs of elimination are also part of this chakra, as well as the navel chakra.

BALANCING THE ROOT CHAKRA

To restore balance in the root chakra, use positive thoughts combined with crystals and gemstones to reconnect with health, wealth, vitality, and well-being. Health, wealth, vitality, and well-being are inherent within you, and it is up to you to reconnect with these resources to manifest them in your life. Below is a list of states of being and consciousness that often accompany an imbalance in the root chakra. The gemstones assist in bringing the change you want to see. If you are agitated or angry, bring balance by using more blue and green gemstones. Feeling weak and unmotivated? Use the motivation vibration of reds.

Anger and Agitation

Add blue stones to offset the overabundance of red energy. Azurite, sodalite, lapis lazuli, angelite, turquoise, and chrysocolla are recommended.

Depression

Add red stones to bring more passion into your life. Use garnet and ruby. Yellow stones like citrine, golden calcite, and yellow topaz work with the energy of the solar plexus, where depression often resides (this will be addressed further in chapter 4).

Inflammation

Chrysocolla calms inflammation and is helpful after surgery. Use chrysocolla, sodalite, and lapis lazuli to reduce the angry red energy of burns and relax spasms associated with menstrual cramps.

Prosperity and Abundance

Ruby gives the impetus to take action. It takes action to make money and create prosperity. Ruby provides the fire and vital energy to motivate and maintain a pace toward attaining a goal. Pyrite, also known as fool's gold, provides grounding, focus, and self-confidence.

Protection

Black tourmaline deflects negativity. Use hematite to create a shield or force field when feeling unsafe or vulnerable. Hematite is also beneficial for protection because the shiny, metallic nature of the stone deflects away feelings or thoughts.

Lack of Focus and Scattered Thinking

Hematite is metallic and grounding. It brings immediate focus and calm. I've seen this stone work with young children during times when they seem to be bouncing off the walls. Place the hematite in their hands to play with and watch the immediate results. Other stones that are effective for grounding are smoky quartz, black tourmaline, and black obsidian.

Weakness, Procrastination, and Laziness

Add red stones to boost energy. Garnet, ruby, and red jasper used with intention can help motivate you.

Gemstones for the Root Chakra

Positive affirmations for each gemstone are included below. These affirmations are suggestions to focus on while using the stones for balancing your root chakra. Remember, the stones are tools that will help you amplify your intention and maintain focus.

Agate

Agate comes in many colors. Regardless of the color, agate gemstones are grounding. Use agate with any chakra based upon the color. In the case of the root chakra, red, brown, black, and gray agates are beneficial.

Brown Agate Affirmation: I am grounded and focused. I now follow through with the task at hand. I am grateful for all the support I have in my life.

Black Tourmaline

Black tourmaline deflects negativity. It puts up a force field when used with conscious direction. The invasion of any type of negativity is not an option when black tourmaline is used with conscious intent. I keep one at the front desk at my shop and one at my desk in the office in my home.

Black tourmaline is effective for significantly reducing the effects of electromagnetic frequencies that are being emitted from cell phones and computers. Even the remote control for your TV and cable box emits these frequencies. Incorporate black tourmaline into your household to deflect these harmful energies.

Black tourmaline is grounding. If you have a tendency to be unfocused and scattered in your thoughts and actions, carry or wear black tourmaline until you retrain and rebalance your energy fields. Every time you touch or see the stone, it will help remind you that your intention is to stay focused and grounded.

Place black tourmaline at your feet in a crystal alignment. A crystal alignment is a meditation experience in which a person places various gemstones around the body. Black tourmaline helps draw out negative thoughts, feelings, and emotions through the soles of the feet to be transformed and repurposed.

Black Tourmaline Affirmation: I am protected. All negative energy is automatically deflected away from me. I have a force field of love and well-being around me. I am grounded and able to maintain focus on the task at hand.

Garnet

Garnet activates creative energy and a passion for living. It's a great stone to get you moving and motivated while staying grounded and focused. It removes blocks. Although garnet is available in green, its most common color is red. This red energy motivates you if you have a tendency toward procrastination.

Garnet used with conscious intent reactivates sensual and sexual energy. It is beneficial in increasing the vital life force of the reproductive organs, thereby increasing fertility. Fertility can also be expressed through fertile thoughts, ideas, and creative pursuits. Employ garnet to help manifest your ideas into reality. In a crystal alignment, place a garnet by your knees and add three to four clear quartz points facing out or away from the knees. The clear quartz amplifies the energy of the garnet.

Garnet Affirmation: I have passion for living. I am grounded and focused. I have a healthy, balanced sex drive and sex life. I am fertile with thoughts, ideas, and prosperity.

Hematite

Hematite is grounding and calming. This metallic gray stone is good for someone with a tendency to be scattered and easily distracted. If you go on tangents and can't seem to get back on target, hematite is the stone for you.

Many people use hematite for reducing blood pressure by wearing a hematite ring or bracelet. It is a tool for focusing intention, *not* a replacement for your blood pressure medications. Use it as an addition to your mind-body consciousness of self-healing.

Hematite is great for calming hyperactivity as well. You might try placing hematite between the mattresses of a hyperactive child. Creating a grid of hematite and rose quartz in the bedroom is good for all ages and promotes good sleep. Be creative with establishing a grid. Place hematite tumbled stones under the four corners of the mattress and rose quartz wands, chunks, or tumbled stones decoratively around the room on windowsills, the dresser, and the nightstand.

Hematite combined with rose quartz helps release fears when feeling unsafe or in need of protection and fills the void with loving energy. Use this visualization: imagine that you are inside a rose quartz sphere enveloped in its loving vibration. Add a layer of hematite on the outside of that sphere, like the outer shell of a piece of candy. The hematite layer deflects negativity and creates a force field. The only option inside the rose quartz sphere is the vibration of love.

Hematite Affirmation: I am calm and relaxed. My muscles are smooth and relaxed. I have perfect blood pressure. Everything is okay and will be okay in the future. There is nothing to worry about. All is well.

Jasper

Jasper can be used at the solar plexus, navel, or the root chakra, depending on the color and your intention. It occurs in shades of red, brown, orange, and yellow. Jaspers come variegated, brecciated, picturesque, and mottled. This stone is grounding and helps you maintain focus. It is also a stone of protection, motivation, and creativity.

Red jasper can activate and move the energy of the root chakra. It stimulates creativity and taking action as you use it with your intention. Dalmatian jasper is predominantly white with black spots, just like the namesake dog breed. It elicits loyalty, energy, and balancing of the yang and yin—the masculine and the feminine, or active and passive, principles. Yellow jasper brings forth the gut feeling of knowing you are safe, protected, and free to be who you truly are.

Red Jasper Affirmation: I am grounded and focused. I am motivated to get up and accomplish all that needs to be done.

Dalmatian Jasper Affirmation: I have exuberant energy. My masculine and feminine energy are in balance. I am grateful for all my loyal friends and family. I am a good and loyal friend.

Obsidian

Obsidian is volcanic glass that naturally occurs in igneous rocks. It has been used to make arrowheads, spear tips, and other tools by various cultures including Stone Age, Mesoamerican, and Native American cultures. The most common colors are black, brown, and seafoam green.

You can find black obsidian in tumbled form, as arrowheads, and as nodules called Apache tears. All black obsidian aids in setting up a protective vibration. There is a reflective quality in all forms of obsidian because it is glass and mirrors energy. The mirror deflects incoming energies to protect you and your property. I have used black obsidian wands in the corners of rooms throughout a building to set up a force field with the intent to dissipate the power of a person whose intent was not for the highest good of participants in a workshop. It worked subtly and effectively.

Apache tears are beneficial when you are grieving a loss of any kind. Tears are helpful in the grieving process on a physiological level. They balance the emotions yet promote healthy crying to release the sadness of the loss.

Black obsidian has several attractive variations. Snowflake obsidian has white snowflake-like markings, reminding you that there is always light within the darkness. The snowflake variety balances the masculine and feminine energy. The black is the feminine, passive, or receptive energy and the white is the masculine, active energy.

Rainbow obsidian has colors streaming throughout it. This stone is a perfect representation of black, containing all the colors of the rainbow, just as white has the full spectrum within it. The rainbow is reflective within the dark black. It shows the colors within the black, which at first glance is dense and dark. Just as you cannot see your chakra system or the rainbow of your subtle body, they still exist. Rainbow obsidian is a tool for remembering all that you are.

The golden sheen in golden sheen obsidian is formed from little bubbles that occur during the lava flow's cooling process. The sheen within the black obsidian offers an additional reflective quality that deflects negativity. This kind of obsidian is good for protection and is helpful if you are around argumentative people. Golden sheen obsidian is a tool that can be used to observe yourself while realizing that all that happens around you is simply a reflection. Observing what occurs outside of and around you helps you grow. Be aware of your inner thoughts, feelings, emotions, and belief systems. Put another way, this stone offers a reminder that when you point a finger at someone else, you have three fingers pointing back at you.

Black Obsidian Affirmation: I am safe. I easily dissipate anything that is unlike love. I find the good within. I am protected. All is well.

Snowflake Obsidian Affirmation: I am able to see the good in the most challenging situations. I can see the light at the end of the tunnel when things seem unbearable. I know there is always hope and help to pull me through in moments that feel like the dark night of my soul.

Rainbow Obsidian Affirmation: I sense all the colors of my being and know they are aligned and balanced. I remember that there is a full spectrum of light—a rainbow—even when everything appears to be dark or challenging.

Golden Sheen Obsidian Affirmation: I am aware of my inner thoughts and feelings. I know people, places, and situations are somehow a reflection of me, and I learn from the mirror. I create my own reality. I am safe. There is only goodness, love, and well-being in my life.

Ruby

Ruby is a red-colored gemstone, a member of the corundum variety of gemstones, and is technically a red sapphire. The precise energy of ruby helps the user get moving with passion. It moves energy, and thus is beneficial when you are trying to get motivated. It's an energizing stone that will activate your ability to take action and bring a task or idea to completion. Ruby is beneficial for activating your sensuality.

Ruby Affirmation: I am energized! I live my life with passion. I am self-motivated. It is easy for me to complete any task at hand. I embrace my sensual side.

Essential Oils for the Root Chakra

As mentioned earlier, the root chakra is the place of grounding, passion, abundance, sexuality, sensuality, and our basic survival needs of food, water, and shelter. When root issues are challenged, a high level of stress may result. Stress can cause you to freeze in fear, block the flow of life, and inhibit your ability to consciously create positive circumstances. Being frozen also blocks incoming financial support to meet basic needs. In a relaxed state of consciousness, you can think clearly and receive guidance. It's easier to shift and change the situation. The following three oils are beneficial for calming you down and allowing prosperity and wellness to ensue.

Patchouli

Patchouli has an earthy scent that is good for grounding. It has a balancing effect and can be used for stress-related emotional disorders. A little bit of patchouli is calming and a large quantity of patchouli is stimulating. It can suppress your appetite. I have found that people either love the scent of patchouli or they abhor it—either way, the scent is strong and distinctive. Patchouli is an aphrodisiac as well. Patchouli is beneficial for fungal and bacterial infections, and can be used for athlete's foot. It is an antibiotic, helps eliminate toxins, and aids in substance addictions. As with all essential oils, add it to a carrier oil and place some of the diluted solution on the bottoms of your feet to deliver its healing properties throughout your body. It is a good oil for manifesting abundance. Use visualization along with the power of the scent of patchouli and imagine yourself prosperous, successful, and having plenty of money.

Spikenard

Spikenard is a biblical oil. Mary Magdalene used it on Jesus Christ before he was beaten by Roman soldiers. I still remember the scene and music from the musical *Jesus Christ Superstar*. Growing up in Brooklyn, we often went into the city to see plays; I saw that play three times! Even the movie version of *Jesus Christ Superstar* emphasizes when one of the apostles musically reprimands Mary Magdalene for using the precious and expensive "nard" on Jesus. This oil was said to be carried in an alabaster jar. Spikenard is viscous, so it has a resinous quality. I believe Mary fully knew about spikenard's sedative qualities; it contains valeranone, one of the chemical components in valerian root. This component is a sleep aid and muscle relaxant that is used for stress disorders. If you've taken valerian root in herbal form for stress, sleep, or pain, you know the magnitude of its relaxation benefits.

Vetiver

Vetiver has an earthy, musky smell. It comes from the root or rhizomes of a perennial grass. It makes sense that a root would be beneficial for the root chakra, don't you agree? This oil is good for grounding you and keeping you safe. Vetiver is used for protection. Placing a few drops at a doorway guards the entrance. Use a diffuser to circulate it in your environment to ward off negativity. Vetiver brings prosperity as you visualize abundance in your life while you smell its fragrance. Use the scent as a tool to help you manifest the means to bring forth plenty of money to support you in your basic needs of food, shelter, and water—and beyond. Vetiver balances the hormones and menstrual conditions. It promotes sleep for insomniacs. It is good for circulation and is helpful in reducing stress and fear.

———

The basis of who we are, what we believe, and the creation of the rest of our reality is based on the foundation of the root chakra. It is important to nurture this chakra, clear it regularly, and energize its vitality on all levels—physically, mentally, emotionally, and spiritually. As we go through life, different layers of awareness arise based on experiences. It is beneficial to weed out what no longer serves us to maintain a clear space upon which all chakras may rest. The various tools and information above provide a plethora of choices to assist in the process.

three

ORANGE ENERGY
AND THE
NAVEL CHAKRA

*C*reative life force is located at the navel, just below your belly button. If you are female, your ability to give birth is located at this center. Whether you are giving birth to a child, a book, a new business, or a piece of artwork, the energy of creation comes from the navel chakra. It is the place of fertility and abundance. You can be fertile with thoughts and ideas just as you can be fertile to bring forth children into the world. Your fertile energy is coupled with the fiery passion to bring it to fruition. The impetus to make things happen comes from this orange vibration. The motivation to "just do it!" swirls within the orange color of this center.

The orange energy of the navel chakra is located about three fingers below your belly button. This center is sometimes referred to as the sacral or sexual chakra. The primary color associated with the navel is orange, as well as peach, burnt orange, deep gold, and honey-colored brown. Peach can be used at the navel to bring more pink—specifically love—to the navel. Use rhodonite and rhodochrosite for this purpose. Being friendly, optimistic, and creative, and demonstrating a sense of belonging and the ability to follow your intuition are indications that your navel center is balanced.

THE NAVEL CHAKRA

Primary Colors: Orange, peach
Complementary Colors: Blue, green
Stones: Bloodstone, calcite (including orange calcite), carnelian, chrysocolla, tiger's eye
Other Stones for Balance: Chrysocolla, lapis lazuli, rhodonite, rhodochrosite, sodalite, turquoise
Location: About three fingers below your belly button
Musical Note: D
Essential Oils: Clary sage, jasmine, Margaret's Euphoria blend, orange, sweet marjoram, rose, ylang ylang
Keywords: Activity, creativity, emotions, fertility
Physical Body: Female reproductive organs, kidneys, mammary glands, skin

CHARACTERISTICS OF THE NAVEL CHAKRA

The navel chakra is the energy center where creativity resides. The ability to manifest reality is held here. It's entirely up to you what you wish to manifest; it can be a book, a child, a business, a garden, a delicious meal, a sculpture, and so on. The possibilities are endless. Pull the energy up from the belly to step into action to make it so!

This center is also the center for dreaming. In order to manifest anything, we must be able to see it in our mind's eye—whether in our waking daydreams or our sleeping night dreams. The creative force of dreamtime comes forth from the area of the womb. Many indigenous cultures focus on the navel as the center of power for meditation, dance, and dreaming.

The navel chakra is also a storage center associated with emotions—both positive and negative. Often, emotions we least want to deal with are shoved down deep into the navel chakra. It is the place from which most cords of attachment to people, places, and things of the past must be cut and released.

Fertility

The womb is located at the navel. It is the primary vibration for reproduction and birthing babies onto the planet. Fertility is required to reproduce children. The navel center must be vital, brilliant, and strong in both parents. The father's seed must be strong and have endurance and the ability to bring forth healthy, new life.

Your baby's soul already exists, and parenting begins before conception. If you intend to bring children into the world, take steps prior to getting pregnant to heal your emotional wounds. Both the father and the mother need to become aware of their spiritual, mental, and emotional consciousness along with the physical aspect of bringing a baby into the world. Be conscious in your thoughts and actions with your partner regarding the spiritual love between the two of you, and the higher love you will share with your child. Connect with the sacredness of your lovemaking and the magnitude of the creative act.

Align with the spirit of your unborn child to consciously magnetize your son or daughter to you. Preconception parenting will set the groundwork to be carried throughout your child's life. Ask yourselves what kind of spiritual foundations you wish for your child to have, and begin to establish them prior to conception.

Conscious conception is very rewarding and can open the doorway to making the birth of your child an even more amazing experience. The energy of the navel center also holds the vibration of creativity and giving birth to ideas, not just children. The act of giving birth comes from the father's vibration just as much as it does the mother's. It appears more evident with the woman because she carries the child, yet men give birth in a different way. Intention, energy, foundational strength, and consciousness within the male parent are equally important in bringing forth a sacred being into the world. Just as you align with the spirit of your creation—your child—employ a similar connection to the creation of your reality.

Creativity

The orange at the navel can be used as a focus for the intentional creation of reality. What do you want to give birth to? Connect with the end result in advance. Connect with the spirit of your creation as if it already exists. Do you want to create your own business, build a house, create a garden, or write a book?

Imagine the spirit of your creation. Contemplate these questions: What does it look like? How does it feel? How does it smell? If your creation is something you can hold, imagine not only what it may physically feel like—the sensations as you touch it—but also how it feels to you on an emotional level. Use all your senses: thought, emotion, taste, smell, touch, sight, and sound. Whatever you put your attention on will be created.

To create something, organize your thoughts. Make a list of what you want. Arrange these thoughts into categories like income, career, family, travel, physical, social, education, and spirituality. Written goals and intentions clarify and crystallize your objective. Prioritize, visualize, make lists, and set deadlines. Establishing a deadline creates a chemical reaction in your body, mind, and spirit to make a goal a reality. Use lists to help you stay organized and focused.

Exercise

THE NAVEL MANIFESTATION LIST

On a blank piece of paper, write down one hundred things you would like to manifest or create in your life. Don't hold back. Include all kinds of dreams and wishes. Once you've completed your list, organize your entries into the following categories:

Education
Family/Friends
Income/Career
Physical
Social
Spirituality
Travel

Next, prioritize the entries in each category so that the most important things you desire are at the top. Now, take one or two items from all of the categories and make a to-do list for each of those items, including everything required to make it happen. Establish deadlines for each of the items on your to-do list. Be very specific and work on something on the list every day.

Anything you ardently desire, visualize with passion, truly believe in, and enthusiastically act upon will come to pass.

The navel chakra is the energy center of manifestation. Combine your written lists and visualizations with affirmations. Place a carnelian in your pocket or wear a carnelian bracelet as a constant reminder to keep you on task. Carnelian is orange agate. The orange color activates the natural color of the navel and the agate helps to ground and to keep you on task. Use the fertile thoughts you've planted in your consciousness and water them until they become a reality.

As you move toward consciously creating new circumstances, resistance to change may arise. Underlying emotions that have been lying dormant can crop up.

Emotions

Emotions can get stuck in the navel, especially remnants of mental, physical, and verbal abuse. Sometimes people who have experienced abuse have digestive problems. The navel is physically located at the place where the biological function of elimination occurs. This aspect of digestion from a metaphysical standpoint can be looked at to see what thoughts, feelings, and emotions must be eliminated in order to let new, positive, empowering experiences into our lives.

In addition to the damage of verbal, mental, emotional, and physical abuse stored within the navel, unresolved sorrow and grief can also become stuck in this area. In Chinese medicine, the lung and large intestine share the same meridian, a specific line of energy in the body. The lungs react to grief. If one doesn't express grief through the natural healthy avenue of tears, internal crying results. The internalization may set the stage for certain illnesses. Pneumonia can result during a grieving period. If the grief, sorrow, or negative emotion is unresolved, the energy becomes stuck and stored in the navel. When chronic constipation manifests, be aware that it is time to look deeper into unresolved issues. This looking within, along with proper nutrition, should restore the flow.

Your navel chakra is probably out of balance when find yourself being overly sensitive, distrustful, and self-negating. You may be burying your emotions instead of dealing with them. By employing the self-observation techniques shared in chapter 1, you can adjust your behavior and reactions.

The out-of-balance condition of this chakra can present itself as being emotionally explosive, aggressive, controlling, or having a self-serving attitude. These behaviors are your way of trying to protect yourself and are an unfortunate coping mechanism to prevent remembering or thinking about traumatic events. You may believe that the strong reactions will protect you from anything remotely similar to the negative experiences of the past from happening again. Perhaps on some level, you think you can control the situation. Once you observe yourself trying to control things or become aware of the underlying cause of your reactions, you can then shift to a different place and change your behavior.

Awareness is always the key. Once you have that awareness and observe yourself or even someone else acting in this manner, you will be less judgmental, having more compassion for yourself and others instead of taking their actions personally. As Don Miguel Ruiz shares in his teaching of the Four Agreements, "Don't take anything personally. It's not about you." More often than not, the reactions of others have nothing to do with you.

Reactions are specifically related to what is going on within the person reacting. Practice loving kindness and compassion with yourself. Using a peachy, pinkish-colored stone like rhodonite or rhodochrosite would be helpful in bringing more love into the situation. Both rhodonite and rhodochrosite offer the loving color pink through the shade of peach for integration into this lower chakra. Bringing more heart and more love to you can transform your reactions.

This insight provides more compassion in your interaction with people when they are acting up or emotionally upset. People react in a strong manner because they are unhappy and sometimes haven't acknowledged their unhappiness. The unhappiness may be unconscious and buried deep within. Instead of seeking to be understood, ask how you can understand and have tolerance for the one who is acting out. However, being human means that reactions will arise without warning. This is life. If people didn't have reactions or emotions, it would mean that either all sentient beings have realized enlightenment, or people have become severed from their feelings.

You don't have to fix anything or everything for everyone, or even say much. Often just listening and holding the space for your friends, coworkers, or fellow humans will help them feel better. Be loving and compassionate. Allow the spiritual being that you are see life from a greater perspective.

Clearing Negative Emotions

It's helpful to have mental, emotional, and physical issues cleared so you have a clear slate on which to create your reality. Clear the clutter of your mind and emotions. How can you go about clearing it?

- Observe what needs to cleared. View yourself as an impartial observer without concern as to how you will clear it. Try to remain unattached to your observation. Imagine you are watching a movie you are playing a part in simultaneously. Once you see what the script holds, you can make a choice to change it!

- Seek assistance from a spiritual healer or a counselor to facilitate regression therapy. Regression therapy offers the opportunity to go back to the source of challenges and repetitive negative life patterns you've experienced. Some regressions bring you to a past life. Some regression experiences surprise you and bring you to a memory of something that happened during your first ten years of life.

- Heal the child within. Regardless of how wonderful a childhood you may have had, there are often events that affected you. Even though you are now an adult, when you look back, you understand that as a child, these events had a profound impact on you and flipped a switch in you that affects how you deal with people and situations in your adult life. Now as an adult, spend time with your inner child to heal the original source of emotional and mental issues.

As an example, here is a story from when I was a little girl. I was blessed with an amazingly loving family life. I was about three or four years old. I was playing with children that lived two doors down. The children were making mud pies. I was too little to recognize the pies were made of mud. They made the pies before I entered the scene, so I had no way of knowing, especially at that young age. They convinced me to have a piece of this supposedly delicious chocolate pie. Wow! I took one bite and what a shock! In addition to it being totally disgusting, I was mortified, embarrassed, and felt betrayed by my friends.

As an adult looking back, you might think, "Oh, children will be children, what's the big deal?" but from that moment on, my level of trusting others shifted. It wasn't until I remembered that event and consciously healed the betrayal that I was able to trust myself and others. Of course, it could affect me today if I allowed someone to trick me into believing an untruth or take advantage of my trusting nature. That's part of life. It takes all kinds of people to make this world go around and for lessons to be learned and integrated.

Because I consciously remembered the initial triggering event and healed it from within, situations of a similar nature in adult life don't affect me to the same degree. Every experience we have affects us, regardless of whether or not we are conscious of it. The experiences of life create a cord or energy within our vibrational field. The cord becomes the mechanism for the buttons that get pushed and the reactions we have to life circumstances.

Cut the Cords

You are made of energy. Your energy is composed of strands of power. These strands link you to all the memories, people, and places you've experienced, as well as all your relations. If a beneficial strand (such as one that provided a valuable lesson, for example) becomes weakened or broken, you must repair it! But first, the consciousness must be there to even know the strand is threatened. Strands may be tangled or even attached to something that isn't yours. Take a journey into the depths of your consciousness to find your strands. Meditation techniques and guided imagery journeys are helpful to find parts of yourself that need love and attention.

Events can be stored in other places of the body, such as the solar plexus, but it seems that these are most often stored in the navel. Addictions we have as adults often stem from events that occurred during our formative years. Follow threads all the way back to their origins; they're still attached to you within your consciousness. These strands affect the manner in which you act as well as how you perceive reality. We've all met people who "push our buttons"; once you pull the root that keeps those buttons or strands connected, you can heal the wounds and move on to a happier and more productive life. Then when those buttons are pushed, you won't be affected because they are disconnected!

Journeys into the self to retrieve energy and cleanse it are wonderful tools—they can be used for all issues residing at any chakra. Emotional and mental issues are a bit more challenging and harder to retrieve when buried at the navel chakra. Journeys help you banish your doubts and embrace the full potential of your being because you know yourself better. They provide you the opportunity to know the source of the challenge so you can release and cleanse it from your consciousness. Taking a journey within allows you to open your heart and follow a higher path.

I have seen amazing results with clients who have become conscious of these varying levels of hurt, betrayal, or emotional scarring. Getting the metaphorical piece of sand out of your eye can really change the way you see.

Dreaming

When I trained with a medicine woman in dreaming and stalking techniques, she would have me dream from my navel. To dream from my navel, I would form a strong intention to dream from my navel. Prior to falling asleep, I placed a river rock on my navel. The river rock was flat and bigger than a large baking potato. Placing a river rock on my navel drew my attention to that energy center and reminded me of my intention to dream from that center as I fell asleep. I was blessed with many profound dreams using this technique. Much of this training was based on the teachings of Carlos Castaneda. Castaneda was an author who wrote a series of twelve books, starting with *The Teachings of Don Juan* in 1968. Two of these techniques are dreaming and self-stalking, the latter of which is explained in the next chapter.

In many cultures, the navel is considered a place of power, a dreaming center, and a focus point for manifestation. It is an energy center where intuition dwells. You have probably heard of "going with your gut," a saying that stems from the knowledge that your feelings of intuition are physically located in the band of energy at the navel region.

The navel chakra is the place where memories, feelings, and emotions are stored. These memories create the basis from which you perceive reality, and includes both positive and negative thoughts, feelings, and emotions. Use the vibrational energy of the navel and dream from this chakra center. Dream big, and believe that anything and everything is possible. Feel your dream, and act as if your dream is already a reality.

Body Parts Related to the Navel Chakra

The physical parts of the body directly related to the navel chakra are the skin and kidneys, two major organs of elimination. To maintain a balanced navel, you must release what has been processed and is no longer needed on physical, mental, and emotional levels. The mammary glands and the female reproductive organs are energetically connected with this chakra, as it is the place of reproduction and creation.

BALANCING THE NAVEL CHAKRA

Below is a list of states of being and consciousness with corresponding gemstones that assist in bringing about the change you want to see in your life. Remember, if you have buried emotions deep down and the thought of dealing with them scares you, don't use more orange; instead, rebalance the chakra by bringing in more blue and green stones. If you tend to avoid dealing with emotions, add orange in order to light the proverbial fire under yourself.

Buried Emotions

Elestial quartz crystals are great tools for delving deep within to get to what's buried. These crystals are also known as water crystals because they are usually found in riverbeds. The watery nature of this gemstone lends itself well to connecting with your emotions, as emotions are ruled by the element of water in your consciousness. Smoky quartz is also a beneficial stone for this chakra to seal and heal a buried emotional wound. The wound is an energetic hole. The smoky quartz grounds, protects, and seals the energetic hole when used with conscious intent. Use malachite's swirling nature and green healing energy to aid in balancing the vibration of soreness left from the emotions.

Creativity

Add orange and darker shades of yellow stones to activate the vibration of creativity. Mental clarity is necessary to allow for the visionary stream of consciousness to come through. Use carnelian, orange calcite, and citrine to bring through creativity and to release mental blocks.

Dreaming

People often tell me they don't dream. If you sleep, you dream. There are forms of dreaming which occur in the deepest sleep (REM sleep), and there is also lucid dreaming, a form of conscious dreaming which can occur when you are in twilight sleep. Dreams can serve as inner psychologists. In addition to restoring vital energy during sleep, the subconscious is busy working through various issues and situations that arose throughout the day. It's a time for the physical body and the mind to catch up with each other and process and integrate all that has occurred. Daydreaming, which occurs while awake, is a valuable tool to awaken consciousness to various potential realities. Herkimer diamonds and amethyst crystals are useful in helping to remember dreams and the various dreaming states. Herkimer diamonds are very energizing and can be used to stimulate lucid dreaming.

Fertility

Breathe more orange into your navel to activate the vibration of fertility. Imagine the sun as it sets, casting an orange hue on the horizon. Take that image and breathe the color into your navel. Use carnelian, red jasper, and red goldstone to remind you of that color vibrating at exactly the right rate within and around you.

Self-Negation

Amber is a great stone for learning how to establish boundaries with others and raise your personal power. Dark orange citrine, orange calcite, and golden calcite assist you in finding the part of you that remembers that you are worthy and magnificent.

GEMSTONES FOR THE NAVEL CHAKRA

Positive affirmations for each gemstone are included below. These affirmations are suggestions to focus on while using the stones for balancing your navel chakra. Remember, the stones are tools that will help you amplify your intention and maintain focus.

Bloodstone

Bloodstone is a popular stone for assisting new mothers in childbirth. When used with conscious intention, it helps regulate blood flow and relaxes the muscles just enough to make a less painful delivery. This stone is also good for the blood. It is mostly green with specks of red. Use it at the lower two chakras in a crystal alignment. Regardless of whether you are a man or a woman, everyone births things into reality. So whether you are having a child or birthing a business, relationship, or piece of artwork, bloodstone can be used when you are ready to deliver your creation into the world.

Bloodstone Affirmation: I easily birth my creation into the world. My blood is healthy and circulates just as it should.

Calcite

Calcite occurs in orange, blue, honey, brown, green, pink, red, and colorless. The orange and honey varieties are beneficial at the navel chakra. Calcite appears in different forms like masses or chunks, rhomboid, and dogtooth formation. Dogtooth calcite is the gemstone found in crystal caves forming stalactites and stalagmites. Calcite is a crystal that twins with other crystals. Sometimes this crystal twinning is simply by contact or by penetration with another crystal. I have often seen calcite attached to amethyst.

Calcite twinning provides the vibration of support and synergy. With this in mind, orange calcite helps calm muscle spasms, relax back pain, and restore balance to ligaments and tendons. After all, it is our muscles, back, and ligaments that support our physical body. Balance is achieved through use of the stone in meditation and the visualization of restored health and well-being. Orange calcite realigns the emotions and assists in rebalancing the navel chakra.

Calcite has the ability to assist you when you're going through change. Change is the only thing that is constant in your life, right? Using calcite anytime, then, can be helpful. Essentially, calcite helps shift the anxiety associated with change. That anxiety is simply the fear of the unknown. Although calcite is a mineral, there is a sort of softness about it.

Calcite Affirmation: Change is good. I easily transition into this next chapter of my life.

Orange Calcite Affirmation: I am grateful to have balanced emotions. My bones and muscles are strong and feel good in my body.

Carnelian

Carnelian is an orange agate that can be used for fertility and reproduction. For those of you thinking you want to stay far away from this stone because you believe it only pertains to actual children, guess what? You can still use it! This stone allows fertile ideas to arise and creativity to flow. With conscious intention, carnelian supports you to birth those creative projects. Your project birthing may include having a fertile life and allowing yourself to give birth to all your desires.

For those of you who want the stone to help you to have a child, through whatever means, keep carnelian close by and imagine your life as if you are already the mother or father of your wonderful child. Use your creative imagination and dream it into reality on the orange ray of carnelian.

Carnelian is helpful for those suffering with arthritis. Take the action of ridding your body of the wastes that created the arthritis on a physical level. Rid your mind of the limiting belief systems regarding hereditary diseases and the reversal of certain affectations. For example, if your family has a history of arthritis, you can make a conscious choice to break the pattern. You can decide not to accept the potentiality of having the health challenge. Become aware of the emotions stuck in your joints to allow them to be released. Carnelian helps to maintain awareness. Combining the awareness with healthful eating habits reverses the potential for the arthritis to manifest. Use carnelian to birth a new reality with easy, flowing joints free of inflammation.

Carnelian Affirmation: I breathe easily and know that all is well. I take in a deep breath of life and breathe out in a relaxed, even flow. *To release arthritis:* All my joints are healthy and comfortable. I release all anger in a healthy, balanced way. All toxins are easily processed and removed from my body. *For fertility:* We are fertile and easily able to reproduce a beautiful, healthy child.

Chrysocolla

Although chrysocolla is a blue-green stone, it is beneficial for balancing the energy at the navel chakra. This stone can be used at any chakra for restoring balance. Chrysocolla contains azurite, malachite, and cuprite. Together, these stones create a team effective at calming aggravation and inflammation.

With conscious direction, chrysocolla is a tool aiding in healing abuse, anger, and cancer. Chrysocolla is the stone to turn to when you are dealing with the more difficult issues buried in your consciousness. Although deeply buried, these issues raise their ugly heads when certain things happen that push your buttons. You may find yourself reacting to someone or something that makes no sense to you. Sometimes these issues keep coming up and you can't understand why they continually occur throughout your life in various but similar ways. The names and faces may change, but the patterns or challenges are the same. Grab chrysocolla and sit in meditation or with a journal and intend on uncovering whatever "it" is that needs to be worked through and healed.

This stone is good for keeping inflammation and bleeding down when you have to undergo an operation or dental work. Remember, you can always envision a crystal, reenvision its energy, and surround your loved one with this stone's vibration even if you don't have it with you.

Chrysocolla can be a woman's best friend during the challenging yet powerful cycles of menstruation and menopause. It alleviates hormonal challenges and calms inflamed states of consciousness. Use the calming vibration of the blue-green stone to cool off the power surges.

Chrysocolla Affirmation: I am calm and at peace. My body is healthy and balanced. My body naturally reduces inflammation that is not for my highest good. My cells naturally regenerate and rejuvenate to maintain a healthy, balanced body. My hormones are balanced. I accept the nurturing vibrations of Mother Earth.

Tiger's Eye

Tiger's eye has a luminous, reflective effect like a sheen or a shimmer. The most common colors of tiger's eye are golden brown, red, and blue. The reflective quality is what contributes to its ability to deflect negativity. Tiger's eye can be used to keep away negative thought-forms, regardless of whether those thoughts are yours or belong to someone else. This stone is often used as an amulet to ward against the evil eye.

Use red tiger's eye to motivate you to take necessary action to bring projects to completion and realize the benefits of hard work, and to instill high self-esteem, courage, insight, and foresight combined with the vital energy to make it so!

Golden Tiger's Eye Affirmation: I am safe. I am confident and aligned with my personal power. I set boundaries easily.

Red Tiger's Eye Affirmation: I am vital and energetic. I am self-motivated and create the world I want to experience.

ESSENTIAL OILS FOR THE NAVEL CHAKRA

The navel chakra is your connection to your creativity and your fertility. Fertility is the natural ability to give life. You have the natural ability to give life to ideas. This capability involves relaxed yet motivated action to complete the goal at hand. Removal of toxins and emotionally stuck energy must be removed to balance this chakra.

Clary Sage

Clary sage is helpful for the navel chakra and the solar plexus, as well. It is extremely beneficial as an antidepressant. As a navel chakra oil, it is a uterine tonic and is said to be beneficial for fertility (perhaps because it is an aphrodisiac) and balancing the hormones. Clary sage is a mild sedative and creates a euphoric state. It reduces blood pressure, too, so don't use it if you plan on having a few drinks, as you could have an adverse reaction.

I created a blend for PMS or menopausal symptoms for women. It has clary sage as its primary note with secondary notes of lavender, geranium, and spikenard. This is a synergistic, proprietary blend. These oils help to realign the intense mood swings and tension that is often caused by stress, PMS, or menopause. Remember, clary sage lowers your blood pressure, so if your pressure is already low, you should probably stay away from it. Feel free to create your own version using these oils or other essential oils with similar effects.

I used the Euphoria blend when I had to have a biopsy taken from my left breast. At the time of the procedure, I didn't know the mass was benign. The synergistic blend helped me remain calm during the procedure and the ensuing days as I waited for the results. The spikenard in the blend helped as well because of the valeranone.

Jasmine

Jasmine is used as an aphrodisiac and for fertility. It is also used for childbirth and to relieve women's reproductive problems. The scent directly affects the emotions and is calming. ˙

Orange

This citrus oil is beneficial for the navel, as it comes from the same color vibration as the color of the chakra. It is uplifting and pulls you out of depression because of the sunny vibration associated with oranges. It is known for balancing movement of the navel area, including the bowels, whether diarrhea or constipation. It also helps with the digestion of fats and may be beneficial for lowering cholesterol.

Rose

Rose oil is beneficial as an aphrodisiac and to improve fertility. Rose relaxes you when you are tense or in an emotional crisis. Rose oil may be used for skin care, for circulation, and in childbirth. Rose is an eternal symbol of love and is also a heart chakra oil. (Read more about rose oil in chapter 5, on the heart chakra.)

Sweet Marjoram

This oil may be used for any and all of the chakras. I associate it foremost with the navel chakra, since the angst you hold is often found buried in the navel area. It helps alleviate crying, anxiousness, hysteria, paranoia, and the feeling of needing protection. It allows you to relax, release stress, and easily deflect negativity. It helps to rid headaches and clears respiratory challenges. Sweet marjoram is an essential oil you can add to a blend for muscular aches or muscle spasms. It is helpful for insomnia and may make you sleepy.

If you feel you need extra protection because you are around a lot of negative people, place some sweet marjoram on your temples and the back of your neck.

Ylang ylang

Ylang ylang is helpful for balancing irritability, PMS, and nervous tension. This oil will also reduce blood pressure. It relaxes the nervous system and can be beneficial for overcoming anxiety, shock, fear, and panic. Ylang ylang is also an aphrodisiac and balances hormones. Those two qualities alone help to align the navel chakra.

———

There are many tools available to balance the emotions, release underlying patterns, and create your life. What gemstones and essential oils have you determined will be best to assist you at this moment in your life? Are you ready to step up to the plate and create? Pick a stone and start the process today! After reading about the navel chakra, you should be all fired up and enthused to just do it!

four

YELLOW ENERGY
AND THE
SOLAR PLEXUS CHAKRA

*T*he sun shines brightly with golden yellow rays of light just below your heart, so take off your sunglasses and let your light shine! The place between the heart and the navel is called the solar plexus. The main color associated with the solar plexus is yellow. Shades of green, such as olive, emerald, forest, and chartreuse, strengthen and balance the solar plexus. This center regulates your ability to digest life, digest food, stand in your personal power, establish healthy boundaries, recognize your magnificence, and live your life with self-confidence. The ability to truly stand in your own brilliance, do or achieve anything you put your attention on, and become anyone you want to be is established during the first ten years of your life.

The solar plexus is the center for your ability to take in, absorb, and integrate life and all it offers—the good as well as what you may perceive as the bad. The solar plexus manages the vibration of experiencing and digesting all you see and experience around you and in your life. It can be compared to the powerful and amazing sun shining brightly in the sky. The brilliance of light at this center brings mental clarity and the ability to see life from a greater perspective. It's a great visual to imagine the sun shining at your solar plexus to warm you up and integrate all that life has to offer.

THE SOLAR PLEXUS CHAKRA

Primary Colors: Yellow

Complementary Colors: Green, olive, purple

Stones: Amber, apatite, citrine, golden calcite, goldstone, jasper, malachite, peridot, tiger's eye

Other Stones for Balance: Amethyst, charoite, purple agate, sugilite

Location: Between your heart and your navel

Musical Note: E

Essential Oils: Anise, bergamot, fennel, lemon

Keywords: Intelligence, mental clarity, personal power, self-esteem

Physical Body: Adrenals, breath, diaphragm, digestive organs, skin

CHARACTERISTICS OF THE SOLAR PLEXUS CHAKRA

Self-confidence and self-esteem are the keywords for this energy center. The opposing force to our self-confidence are things like self-sabotage, shyness, depression, and the fear of being all that we can be. Many of us have background programs running, telling us that our best isn't good enough, so why even bother trying? Well, I say "pooh" to that—it's simply an excuse. If the people of the world who have achieved great things and helped many people said these same things to themselves, where would we all be right now?

It has become apparent that many people are walking around with thoughts of not being good enough and a fear of failing. Delve into this chapter on the solar plexus to heal these issues once and for all. Do it for yourself and for all beings!

Self-Confidence

With a balanced solar plexus, you see and live in the world with joy, optimism, and a positive attitude. And when you are filled with joy, it is easy to be enthusiastic, self-confident, and courageous. It takes courage to shine your light brightly.

It is important to shine your light, because this encourages others to do the same. It is a selfless act as you become a role model. To encourage is to inspire someone else to have courage and confidence. Your ability to encourage encompasses holding a vision and believing in the goal. To be encouraging involves holding the space for someone to be confident or hopeful.

When you believe in yourself, you can achieve great things and make a difference in the world. Having self-confidence propels you forward to achieve your heart's desires. Your belief in yourself helps many other people and provides a service to the world, your community, and your own family. It benefits no one to play small or incapable.

To dare to step forth when afraid; to live passionately; to be present and uphold relationships in life, love, and work is what being in this world is all about. It takes courage and self-confidence to go out and create, step forward, and be counted.

I have a perfect example of this in my own life. After the stock market crashed in 1987, my successful mortgage banking career ended simultaneously with a long-term, committed relationship. I was devastated. It took tremendous courage to pull myself out of depression, and it took even more courage to open my shop, The Crystal Garden, when I knew nothing about running a retail store.

Yet the result of having the courage to step into the unknown to follow my dream resulted in many years of helping many people. What appeared to be a retail store ended up being a sanctuary for thousands of people. In a sense, my courage enabled me to pay it forward to so many others in need of encouragement, help, love, and spiritual fulfillment.

Self-Sabotage

Why do you sometimes sabotage yourself by doing a half-finished job? What keeps you from living your dream? What prevents you from being the best you can be at all times? Is there an inner voice telling you that you're not good enough? What's the source of that voice? Do you actually believe those negative echoes of things repeated to you from your past?

Get to the source of the self-sabotage, accept it, heal it, and move on. This requires delving into the underlying cause of the sabotage, and it is where you use the tool of self-observation (from chapter 1) to note your thoughts and belief systems. Use the recapitulation exercise in chapter 2 to pinpoint the moment in time when the belief started. Applying these tools will help you uncover the source of your self-sabotage and you'll be able to overcome the challenge. You could even use that old source as a challenge to fire you up to prove that it's wrong. On some level, you have already proven that none of those words or actions have any truth or validity anymore, so why let them continue to hold you back?

While delving into the source of current life challenges, look at whether or not you had encouragement from adults during your developmental years. A multitude of experiences that occurred in your childhood may affect you well into your adult years. They remain in your subconscious until you uncover them and self-heal.

The result of childhood experiences could make you do an impeccable job because you are still trying to prove a point. For example, I remember when I was about ten years old and working on my math homework at the dining room table. My father came home, and I told him I was having a hard time doing the math. He responded, "Well, if you can't do math, you'll never be a banker." I think it hadn't occurred to me to be a banker until that moment in time. In retrospect, I realize my father's statement made a great impact on me. As a result, I became a regional senior vice president of a major mortgage banking company by the age of twenty-seven.

The opposite effect of childhood experiences is self-sabotage, fulfilling those misguided beliefs of not being good enough. Every word, feeling, and action affects you in your formative years. The effect is either a need to prove the echoes of those positive voices wrong or prove those negative voices right.

In the next exercise, and throughout this book, I speak of "self-stalking." If you've had a stalker, or known others who have, the term might make you feel a little uncomfortable. I understand your concern in using the term "stalking," and I wish to address it. "Stalking" is used in Toltec teachings and is a process that dramatically demonstrates the energy associated with uncovering the true source of emotional, mental, physical, and spiritual challenges.

In fact, if you're feeling uncomfortable with the thought of "stalking yourself," I invite you to use that vibration as a tool. Just as it's uncomfortable to have a tooth drilled when you have a cavity, it must be done to prevent infection and for that tooth's (and your whole mouth's) health. Likewise, use this metaphorical "drill" to remove what needs to be discovered, illuminated, or addressed directly, in order to make the space available and replace what no longer serves you. It may be painful, but the "drill" will help you transform your life in a positive way, using your thoughts, feelings, and intentions.

You can look back at the unfortunate time in your life when you were stalked to uncover anything else that was going on with your family, with your friends, or in your consciousness. Through the use of recapitulation and perspective, you can use your imagination to remove the stalker experience while reflecting on what else was going on at the time. Were you emotionally distressed or unhappy with your life, job, or relationships? Were you unhappy with your thoughts, feelings, and emotions? Were you feeling like a victim? Remember, do this self-examination review as if the stalking was not happening. See what you uncover.

Exercise

STALK YOURSELF

This simple exercise will bring greater awareness in all parts of your life. Memories will arise and old thought-forms will offer you the opportunity to heal childhood issues in a safe and comfortable way. Repetitive statements and programs were imposed upon you as a child. To improve your self-confidence, remove the statements and underlying programs that aren't true—and probably never were. Are you ready to increase your awareness?

This exercise is a meditation-type experience. Try it on your own as a tool for self-discovery. Again, keep some paper or journal and a pen nearby, and turn off your phone.

Take a look at yourself and your life. Is there a repetitive pattern that is a theme in your life? Are you experiencing the same types of relationships over and over again at work, at home, in all aspects of life? Stalk yourself. Watch yourself like a tiger watches its prey. Observe your actions and reactions to circumstances without judgment. Now decide one issue in your life you are ready to release or heal. Set an intention for this exercise.

Rest comfortably in a reclining position. Decide you are going to trust in the process. You really can't do this wrong. Place all your awareness on your breath—on the inhalation and the exhalation.

Be aware of your hands and how your spine supports the structure of your body. Close your eyes and breathe. Observe the expansion of your body when you inhale and observe the contraction of your body as you exhale. If thoughts arise in your mind, observe them and put them on hold.

As you continue to focus on your breath, let yourself relax. Relax every part of your body, starting with your feet. Simply think to yourself and take a deep breath with each of these thoughts: Feet relax. Legs relax. Hips relax. Internal organs relax. Torso relax. Back muscles relax. Shoulders relax. Arms and hands relax. Face and scalp relax.

Put all of your awareness on the center of your forehead and then the center of your chest, near your heart. Breathe in and breathe out. Imagine you are walking in the door of a house—any house. Whatever house comes to mind, walk in the door and go into a room that you are attracted to.

Observe who is in the room.

Allow your imagination to expand. Give yourself permission to make it up. It is the key to a powerful experience.

Trust who you see, sense or feel nearby you in that space.

Are you a younger you? If you were to pick a number, an age between one and ten—what number would you choose?

Become that age and look through the eyes of yourself at that age.

Who is near you and what do you feel?

Remember the intention you set when you started the exercise.

Observe how you feel and what is happening around you. It doesn't matter if you feel like you are making everything up. Trust the process and let the experience evolve.

In fact, as you read this exercise in preparation for the meditation experience, you may have already started seeing, sensing, remembering, or feeling something that will jar the emotion that is directly associated with the underlying program that thwarts your self-esteem. Notice it. Write it down. And let yourself recognize that this program is not your truth. It was the truth of the person you may have respected or who was an authority figure in your life at that time.

As you come out of the experience, either write down or contemplate what you would tell your younger self if you were able to travel back in time to help yourself as a youngster. Become the adult helping the younger version of yourself and provide that young child with perspective and counseling.

Through the increased awareness and the self-healing of inner-child work, you will find a natural and easy shift to heal many self-esteem issues as you stalk yourself in different situations at varying ages of your life. Decide what is true and become all that you can be!

Be Recognized and Acknowledged

All that you are, all that you do, and all that you can be is between you and Spirit. No other opinion or comment from anyone other than inspiration from angels or yourself really matters. Your personal truth is about being in alignment with your own integrity and always doing your best. When you do your best, people have a tendency to want to imitate or copy your successes and the way you do things. Sometimes this is perceived as "stealing your ideas," but actually, copying and imitating what someone else is doing is one of the greatest forms of flattery.

There are few new ideas rolling around that people actually connect with in our ordinary existence. Much of what you have learned and used has been copied from others. Often there is a connection with ancient teachings and traditions handed down through the centuries. Even the ideas, words, concepts, and spiritual principles in this book have been said before in many ways by many others. Don't be bothered by someone who is copying you, and certainly don't let the fact that someone else has said or done something before you stop you from implementing an idea, project, or strategy. Instead, take the initiative to go, do, and be your best. When someone emulates you, accept is as a compliment. Be happy they were inspired by you. Remember, you probably copied it or learned it from someone before you. You may have learned it from your parents, a teacher, a book, the movies, or even an ancient civilization.

There is nothing wrong with wishing and wanting people around you to recognize and acknowledge you; it's a natural human tendency. Encourage your friends, family, acquaintances, and strangers. Tell people you are grateful for their contribution to society. Take the time to tell a coworker or employee or even your boss that you appreciate the job they've done. Encourage children and create an environment so they can feel good about themselves, and feel safe, loved, and nurtured. Encourage children to make new friends and have courage.

Your belief in yourself helps many other people. It provides service to the world, the community, and your own family. So, what does it take to have good self-esteem without getting stuck in a big, fat ego and caught up in self-importance? Mentoring from a loved one helped me. The echoes of my mother's voice still assist me when I am getting too big for my britches! To this day, I still can hear my mom say, "SPS, Margaret!" when I get too full of myself. What is SPS? Self-Praise Stinks! But at the same time, I can also feel the echoes of how proud she is of me and the person I have become. One of the many gifts my mother gave me was to believe in myself and acknowledge and recognize my achievements with humility. There is a balance between self-confidence, positive self-talk, and an overbearing ego. Allowing the confidence to shine through brings out the ability to do your best.

Always Do Your Best

Do your best and really step up to the plate to complete tasks with pride in your work—such efforts will not go unnoticed. Your good contributions to the world make an impact on many lives. If you need a reminder of this, watch the Christmas classic *It's a Wonderful Life*. Nothing goes unnoticed. Spirit knows. Your angels know.

Live with passion and vigor! Activating the yellow energy at your solar plexus helps you do this. There have been times when I've been criticized for having an abundance of passion and vigor for my work and in my life. But it doesn't stop me! I'd rather live my life authentically. Shine your light rather than letting it dim out of fear of being judged, or the concern that someone else might feel small. Let go of the fear of living and be in truth as you happily play on this great planet. The sun will shine brighter, the grass will look and smell greener, the birds will sing as they always have, but perhaps you will hear them in a different way. And maybe, just maybe, the courage to be who you truly are will inspire someone else to have the courage to do the same.

As an Italian growing up in New York, my family and friends always did everything with great passion. We felt to the depth of our being. If we had anger, we expressed it—and sometimes quite loudly. Being secure in the love between us allowed us to express our anger and then be done with it. We kissed, hugged, and continued to love each other. There was no judgment or holding grudges. If we cried from sorrow, often it was so deep that those outside of our culture might have perceived it as being overdramatic. In retrospect, however, I have learned that it is important for us to stay centered and honor our sacred legacies, heritage, and connection with our ancestors.

Have the courage to truly speak and act from your heart. Follow your heart in all that you do. Recognize the good and acknowledge it. Have the self-confidence and self-esteem needed to make a difference. Without these abilities, the potential for depression increases. Just as the vibration of self-confidence and courage is held at the solar plexus, the diametrically opposed vibration of depression is equally possible.

Depression

Depression is partially a lack of self-confidence and self-esteem. When you are depressed, bring in yellow energy; it helps brighten the vibrational field. From my many years of counseling and operating The Crystal Garden, I have seen so many people who lack self-confidence. Keep this in mind when you are facilitating a healing process, as it will provide you with compassion and empathy. The development of good rapport with someone is necessary before he or she will reveal inner vulnerability and lack of self-confidence.

Lack of confidence often stems from verbal, mental, and emotional abuse, and it's truly amazing how well self-esteem issues can be hidden from others. These kinds of issues often stem from a belief of being unworthy. Being timid is one sign of a lack of self-confidence. It still surprises me that many people don't know that they deserve love and abundance. Clients will say they want a loving relationship, and I've asked them flat out, "Do you think you deserve love?" and sadly, their answer is often no. This is when it's beneficial to uncover the source of this belief. Although they may feel or say they don't deserve love, somehow they are jealous of others who have love in their lives; it's clear the love is needed and wanted, but some people don't feel deserving of it.

Jealousy

Jealousy is a mixture of emotions. The thoughts, feelings, and behaviors of sadness, anger, insecurity, and anxiety reside mainly within the lower three chakras. A lack of self-confidence fuels fear and anxiety when we see a friend or rival who is happy, successful, and full of joy. The reaction to this observation often results in feelings of jealousy.

Harboring feelings of jealousy prevents you from getting what those happier people have. The key is to come to terms with why a successful person has all those good things. Observe how they accomplished their success. Instead of judging them, use them as a model and perhaps copy some of their techniques for success, if it is in alignment with your own truth. Do what it takes to raise your self-confidence.

Become conscious and clear away any negative thought patterns associated with lack of self-esteem. Use the tools provided to you for transformation. These thought patterns may have originated earlier in this lifetime or in previous lifetimes. At any time in your life, you can decide to throw out the negative thoughts with conscious intention. These negative thoughts may have you holding on to the belief that you are less than magnificent. After all, this area of your body is where you physically digest and detoxify.

Digestion

Your digestive organs are stored at the solar plexus. The subtle bodies—mental, emotional, and spiritual—digest life at the solar plexus. We are multidimensional beings. The more you realize how everything we see, do, think, taste, touch, and feel affects us on more than just one level, the more conscious you can become. Someone who has digestive challenges on the physical level often has trouble absorbing and taking in some part of their life emotionally, mentally, and spiritually. Once you heal the issue emotionally, mentally, and spiritually, the door to rebalancing the physical challenge is opened. True healing happens on all four levels.

This process of healing on all levels involves becoming more conscious. Become conscious of what you feel and think and how that affects you on all levels. Conscious awareness in all you do requires being present. For example, as you prepare and eat your food, be aware of what you are thinking.

Also be aware of what you are thinking and *saying* aloud as you eat and drink. Everything you say and think affects your reality. Now imagine instilling those thoughts into your food and beverages. You add the dimension of physically ingesting those thoughts.

Instill love in your food and beverages by pausing to fill them with love prior to consumption. Instead of being focused on extraneous thoughts, become really present and aware of eating the food or drink, its texture, and how your body is absorbing nutrients and love. Incorporating this practice provides a venue for healthy digestion and absorption of not only what you consume, but also the thoughts you have about your life.

The solar plexus is the energy center for digestion and absorption of food because of its location in and around the physical body. The pancreas, spleen, liver, and gall bladder are directly associated with the solar plexus. This center is as equally responsible for the proper digestion of life and all it encompasses, as it is the digestion of tangible food. There is always a direct correlation to the intensity of a person's life and digestive challenges. Ask yourself, *What is it about my life I just can't swallow?*

Agita is an Italian verb taken from *agitare*, which means "to agitate." *Agita* also means indigestion or the experience of food that "comes back up." On a metaphysical level, agita also means that someone or something is aggravating you, giving you heartburn or an upset stomach. Agita is commonly used by Italian Americans in the metaphysical sense. Apatite, peridot, and prehnite help rebalance agita, as well as remove sources of the agitation.

The skin is our largest organ of elimination; therefore, it is directly associated with the solar plexus. Waste and toxins are released through the skin. To determine the source or origin of agitation, observe where the skin is releasing toxins and what type of release is it. When viewing a challenge or state of disease, everything is a clue. Each clue will lead you to the source of the irritation. The source could be mental, emotional, physical, or spiritual.

Personal Power

The band of yellow energy around your solar plexus is where you store your personal power. It is also stored in the navel. As I've mentioned earlier, chakras overlap and assist each other. Although it might seem like I'm pigeonholing ways of being, the important information to remember is that all chakras harmonize and interact with one another to create a harmonic vibration.

To have your personal power intact means you are able to set boundaries with others. You are able to speak up for yourself when someone has crossed a line. A balanced solar plexus provides the ability to maintain your sacred space and gracefully establish what is acceptable or unacceptable around you.

For example, let's say you suddenly have a business associate who excessively curses as a normal course of conversation, and has a tendency to put down others without any reason. After it finally sinks in that you've unconsciously invited a colleague who is professionally challenged, you would need to take steps to remove yourself from the interaction. The length of time it would take and the course of action chosen would depend on the business association's importance.

Use amber when you are challenged in this way. As a scent, amber is also beneficial to wear when you are working on establishing boundaries. The complementary color to yellow is purple. Using amethyst assists in transforming and transmuting the situation.

Accept the challenge to maintain your personal power and stand firm in your personal power. Ask for divine guidance from angels and guides to inspire you to select the highest and best course of action. Stay focused on love, compassion, and integrity when taking action to clear out the negative energy of doubts, fears, low self-esteem, unmet expectations, abandonment, betrayals, and so on.

Discernment

If you were to ask yourself, *who am I?* what would your answer be? Spending some time in meditation and contemplation provides insight. As you do this, you may also experience judgment or self-criticism. Please try to simply observe the judgments and move beyond them to self-love and affirm all the goodness you are, thereby building self-confidence. Know yourself, and shine the light of who you truly are.

During this process, become aware of those with whom you spend your time and energy. Do they contribute to the good feelings you have of yourself? Do they mirror parts of you that you judge or dislike? Or are they reflective and in alignment with who you are and where you are going? Do the people you spend time with come from a place of integrity, truth, and finesse? Stop and take the time right now to contemplate and answer these questions.

After a bit of self-examination and truthful observation of those around you, you will probably come to the realization that you no longer wish to associate with certain people. You can diminish your association with grace and nonjudgment by removing the need for dramatic endings. Or if association with someone is inevitable, you can limit the amount of time and energy you share with this person. Discernment falls into the qualities of the yellow vibration of the solar plexus.

Please note that there is a big difference between discernment and judgment. Discernment involves making observations and determining if what you observe is in alignment with who you are. Judgment is nonacceptance of a person or an opinion. You aren't required to align with or agree with everyone. Align and agree with yourself!

Analysis Paralysis

An overdeveloped solar plexus has the potential to create an over-analytical personality. The aura of a person with high intelligence, a genius, or someone who spends a lot of time thinking has quite a bit of yellow in the auric field.

I've had the opportunity to read aura photos. An aura photo is taken with an aura camera, which gives a visual representation of one's bioenergetic state. Aura cameras can measure physiological input based on biofeedback technologies and provide information in a photo through a computer interface system. The photo displays a depiction of a person's aura and chakra system. I find it interesting to see my aura captured on film; it's a good tool for self-observation. Although the aura is invisible to the naked eye, the energy can be displayed through the technology of aura imaging.

Concerning intelligence, when the solar plexus is out of balance you may find yourself a bit challenged in the area of social skills. If you are overly intellectual, you may create blocks in moving forward in life due to "analysis paralysis," a condition of overanalyzing life and not moving forward because of a fear of imperfection. This lack of action often leads to missed opportunities. Opportunity often has a window, and if you don't move right away, the window closes or you can lose your own personal momentum. Analysis paralysis is a delay tactic—a very subtle excuse we use to justify our inaction, easily explained away. Many excuses are always available to you as to why you haven't done something.

With a bit of journaling or self-observation, you will realize that any delay tactic you employ is really due to a lack of self-confidence. Add a purple hue to your energy to establish balance. The purple also transforms and transmutes the frozen-in-time delay into action! Carry an amethyst, charoite, or sugilite with the intention that you want to awaken the courage to step forward and take action.

Body Parts Related to the Solar Plexus

The physical parts of the body directly related to the solar plexus are the diaphragm and lungs, including the breath. The digestive organs—the pancreas, spleen, liver, and gall bladder—are located right in the yellow band of energy at the solar plexus. The skin is also part of this center as an organ of absorption and release. The adrenals are part of this chakra, those glands that produce hormonal adrenaline and give you the fight-or-flight instinct. Worry, stress, and fear deplete the adrenals. Increase your self-confidence and everything will fall into place. A function of this chakra is to take in and absorb life mentally, physically, spiritually, and emotionally. You now know your self-esteem is directly related to these organs, so perhaps you can see why balance is so essential.

BALANCING THE SOLAR PLEXUS CHAKRA

Below is a list of states of being and consciousness that correspond with the gemstones you can use to assist in balancing your solar plexus and the yellow vibration in your aura. If you're feeling down in the dumps, be sure to add plenty of the sunny yellow vibration into your energy field. If you are feeling agitated or having digestive challenges, add greens and purples to realign this center.

Confusion

When your self-esteem isn't intact, your ability to see life clearly is clouded by the pain of past struggles or imposed negative beliefs. Clear stones like citrine, clear quartz, or optical calcite will amplify your intention to bring more clarity into your life.

Depression

There is a direct correlation between a lack of self-confidence and depression. To rebalance your energy field from the effects of depression, take a look at the events that preceded the depressed state. Depression usually follows the loss of love, a job, self-worth, or anything you consider important. Begin your rebalancing process by identifying when the depression first started. Use gemstones with the intention to transform the original cause, which will help restore self-worth. In general, yellow and purple stones will help restore more balance and joy. Use amethyst to transform and transmute the depressed energy in the aura and use citrine to instill joy, confidence, and enthusiasm.

Digestive Challenges

The inability to digest food is directly associated with the inability to digest life. This includes having a hard time swallowing what is happening around you. To bring more balance, use apatite, malachite, peridot, and citrine.

Difficulty Breathing

Metaphorically, the inability to breathe fully and deeply is associated with not being able to live life to the fullest and take a deep breath of life. To improve the depth and fullness of your breath, use visualization while working with carnelian, amber, honey calcite, and rose quartz.

Judgmental and Demanding

Judgmental and demanding people have an inferiority complex, which they overcompensate for and cover up by acting in an intimidating manner. Knowing where this behavior comes from can help you deal with people of this nature. Instead of taking their words personally, realize these people are actually *lacking* confidence, hiding under a gruff exterior. Add citrine, golden calcite, rose quartz, and amber to assist in rebalancing the energy field.

Overly Intellectual

An overly intellectual person may need more purple in their energy field. Add stones like amethyst, purple agate, sugilite, and purple fluorite.

Self-confidence

If you are lacking self-esteem, you could develop an inferiority complex. When this occurs, you might perceive you are being persecuted or left out. When your self-confidence is stable, thoughts of this nature don't even enter your mind. To improve this center's yellow vibrations, add citrine, yellow and honey calcite, imperial topaz, and yellow fluorite.

Gemstones for the Solar Plexus Chakra

Positive affirmations for each gemstone are included below. These affirmations are suggestions to focus on while using the stones for balancing your solar plexus chakra. Remember, the stones are tools that will help you amplify your intention and maintain focus.

Amber

Amber is petrified pine resin. It holds the ancient wisdom of trees. According to Celtic and Druid legends and folklore, trees provide profound spiritual wisdom. Amber helps you connect with your ancestry beyond conscious memory. Bringing conscious awareness aids in deeper understanding of aspects of nature inherent from your familial lineage.

As you heal yourself physically, mentally, emotionally, and spiritually, you also provide healing for all the ancestors standing behind you in time. As you raise your consciousness and heal yourself, you break familial patterns of poor health, abusive behavior, addictive tendencies, and anything not in alignment with love. You also provide the foundation and doorway for the next generations of your family, including any extended family, to have the same benefits from your own self-healing. The work you do to heal yourself and make yourself a better person is actually an unselfish act, as many others benefit from your raising your own personal consciousness. The use of complementary gemstones crystallizes this knowledge into reality.

Amber is beneficial in setting boundaries. As you personally heal, the old emotional state of where you came from will try to suck you back in, because it's familiar and comfortable. Those around you may not be comfortable with your changes, as this might require that they'll have to take a look at themselves. As you change, they'll change because of the natural resonant vibration between you. Their discomfort may cause them to attach to you consciously or unconsciously in an effort to try to keep things the way they have always been.

Here's an example scenario: let's say you've chosen to stop smoking cigarettes. During the process of becoming a nonsmoker, you become aware of underlying emotional issues and take steps to heal those issues. The healing transforms your personality and the manner in which you interact with friends and family—you've become more empowered and self-assured. These changes can cause challenges in various relationships, maybe because your friends and family now have to adjust; perhaps they feel threatened. In some instances, your friends and family may do things to undermine your progress because they want things to return to the way they were.

Use amber to maintain your own energy field and for differentiating your energy field from those of others. Amber essence oil is also good for this.

Amber Affirmation: I easily set boundaries with others. I surround myself with people who respect my sacred space. I am protected from others' thoughts and feelings. I feel nurtured and cared for. I am able to recall past lives when I need deeper understanding of life and its circumstances.

Apatite

This stone is beneficial for digesting and absorbing what you need to maintain health, well-being, and balance on all levels. Just as the name of the stone suggests, it's for balancing your appetite and maintaining the right weight. If you are too slender and have a hard time keeping weight on, it will bring balance. If you are overweight, likewise, it will assist you to bring balance. However, I'd like to emphasize that this stone's focus isn't so much on gaining and losing weight as much as it is on restoring balance, health, and well-being. When used with conscious intention, apatite can help food and nutrients be absorbed and digested properly.

Apatite works on all levels. The manifestation of your desires on the physical plane of existence requires sufficient mental and emotional energy. Therefore, before going on an eating plan to gain or lose weight, take a look at how you are digesting life. Are you able to metaphorically "swallow" and take in all that is happening in your world? Is it too much for you to handle? Do you feel deprived in some way? This kind of awareness must take place on mental, emotional, and spiritual levels. Once you become clearly conscious, true and complete healing can manifest and anchor on the physical level.

Apatite is beneficial to keep near you if you suffer from acid reflux or any digestive challenges. Hold the stone or keep it somewhere nearby to look at and touch to remind you of your process in healing. As I discussed earlier, *agita* literally translates as "feeling agitated." It is also used to indicate indigestion or food "coming up," commonly known as acid reflux. When someone gives me a hard time or irritates me, I exclaim, "Don't give me *agita*!" In other words, don't upset me, and stop giving me a hard time. Set boundaries!

Apatite Affirmation: My digestive system works perfectly. I digest life easily. My appetite is balanced and healthy. My body maintains the perfect weight. The people in my life are supportive and calming.

Citrine

When I explain the solar plexus in a class setting, I often ask, "How many of you think you're the best thing since sliced bread?" Less than 10 percent of the room will timidly raise their hands, too embarrassed to admit their magnificence, and maybe only one person will respond immediately with joy and enthusiasm. The reluctance to admit magnificence is learned, socialized behavior.

Use citrine's golden ray to enliven your solar plexus and boost your ability to acknowledge your magnificence. Citrine helps you to shine your light brightly and be all that you can be with joy, self-confidence, and courage.

Citrine also provides the brilliance to bring mental clarity and clear insight into the potential future reality you are creating. It is a stone of manifestation that can be used for all creative endeavors, and can help writers and artists clear mental blocks.

Citrine can also be used to manifest money. It's known as one of the merchant stones. Use it in conjunction with green aventurine to bring more money into your life. I still have the same citrine and green aventurine sitting in my cash drawer from the day I opened The Crystal Garden twenty years ago. Citrine is the ultimate solar plexus stone. It is beneficial for rebalancing digestive challenges, to reactivate your self-esteem and self-confidence, to enable you to set healthy boundaries, and to maintain clear focus and mental clarity.

Citrine Affirmation: I am courageous and shine my light brightly. I am very good at setting boundaries. I am confident and realize that people honor and respect me. I am a valued person in society. My digestive system works well and is very healthy. I am mentally clear.

Golden Calcite

The bright, sparkling, golden energy of this stone exudes joy and happiness. Golden calcite refracts more light than some of the denser versions of calcite. It helps rejuvenate your self-confidence and courage. It reflects your brilliance. Looking at this stone aids in mirroring your magnificence. As a solar plexus stone, it will remind you to shine your light as brightly as the brilliant sun.

Golden Calcite Affirmation: I am so full of joy! I sparkle and shine my light brightly. I have the courage to be all that I can be.

Goldstone (Red)

Goldstone is actually man-made, and isn't really a stone at all—it's glass made from copper and copper salts. It was first made in the seventeenth century by the Venetian Miotti family, although folklore maintains it was first made by Italian monks. It's been referred to as "monk's gold," even though this name's origin has been lost to history. The exclusive license to make goldstone still resides with the Miotti family. This stone's gold vibration has a natural resonance to wealth, abundance, and prosperity.

There is a starry quality to goldstone that brings inner reflection, as well as a reminder that you are a shining star. Gazing into goldstone reminds you of all you can be and to shine your many talents brightly.

Goldstone comes in red, blue, and green varieties, and all colors provide support for your self-esteem and the solar plexus. The orange-red vibration provides grounding and activates courage and passion for life. It is beneficial for the navel chakra as well as the solar plexus chakra.

Goldstone Affirmation: I shine my light brightly as I live fully and passionately. I sparkle for all to see and am a shining star! I am focused and aligned with balanced emotions.

Jasper

This stone can be used at the solar plexus, navel, or root chakra, depending on its color. I've seen jasper predominantly in shades of red, brown, and yellow. Jasper is grounding, protecting, and helps in maintaining focus. Use the yellow variety to increase feelings of safety to shine your light brightly, and to have the courage to be all that you can be in a very grounded way.

Yellow Jasper Affirmation: It is safe to be myself. My self-confidence gives me the courage to be all I can be. I am focused and grounded, and can achieve great heights.

Malachite

Malachite is helpful for realigning the vibration of the solar plexus to assist its organs and the digestive process. Malachite assists in the ability to take in life's sweetness because of its alignment with the heart chakra. This stone also offers pancreatic support to people with diabetes. Use malachite to release the vibration of diabetes from your energy field. Focus your intent on sending messages of health, love, and well-being to your liver and pancreas as you follow your doctor's instructions.

Become participatory in your health care instead of just masking symptoms. Uncover the reasons beneath the inability to process the sweetness of life in your physical body to aid in healing. Employ your mind, heart, and intention to counteract the effects of days gone by and recognize that *you* are the one who creates your reality. You can change your reality through the Law of Attraction. Simply put, the Law of Attraction is "like attracts like." Your thoughts, words, actions, and deeds attract to your life experiences—all of them. Choose your thoughts carefully and be mindful of your actions. Use malachite to maintain the focus you require to achieve that goal.

Malachite Affirmation: I easily digest all I take in and receive all the benefits. My heart is focused on love, light, and well-being. Even when things appear to be swirling around me, I am able to stay focused. I am able to process and digest all the sweetness life offers me on all levels.

Peridot

Peridot is a green stone also known as olivine. This gem has been identified on the moon and Mars, and in meteorites. Peridot provides perspective from outside your normal reality.

Peridot is good for the wounded healer. A wounded healer, or someone who has suffered wounds of their own, often supports others with similar ailments. They are able to have true empathy for the people in their charge. It's important to support the caregiver who is always helping others. Caregivers and healers often need self-healing and rest.

In indigenous cultures, the wounded healer is someone who has overcome an illness through natural or nontraditional means and is able to provide insight to others. An example of this is the initiation process to become a shaman. In certain ancient cultures, the initiate was intentionally bitten by a venomous snake. The initiate had to overcome the physical poison using spiritual, metaphysical, or magical means to become the wounded healer.

Peridot was quite popular in jewelry made soon after World War II. It assisted soldiers who were returning from the battlefield in reentering society. These men and women had to rebuild their lives after being at war and away from home. For the women at home, peridot was a subtle aid in the integration of their changing roles in society. There was a lot to absorb and integrate—life as they knew it had changed.

Peridot is helpful for digestion on all levels. The green color resembles the color of bile and assists with dealing with anger and jealousy. We've heard the expression of being "green with envy," and peridot is good for people who are jealous or angry, as well as good protection for people who are the targets of such emotions.

Peridot Affirmation: I am able to heal myself on all levels: mental, emotional, physical, and spiritual. I assist others in their healing process with my personal experience. I deflect jealousy. I repel people who are jealous, and attract people who are happy for my good fortune. I have a healthy digestive system. I am able to digest life and all that it brings my way with ease and grace.

Tiger's Eye

Tiger's eye has a luminous reflective quality with a sheen or a shimmer. The most common color of tiger's eye is golden brown. The reflective quality is what contributes to its ability to deflect negativity and has been known historically to keep the evil eye at bay. Use tiger's eye to keep away negative thoughts.

The evil eye is the intention of sending negative thoughts, feelings, or emotions toward someone else. Being brought up in an Italian family, it was common for our family to do things to keep away the *mal occhio*, which roughly translates to "bad eye." The evil eye isn't a supernatural phenomenon; it's nothing more than the envy or jealousy of others' good fortune.

Growing up, I noticed my mother was very cautious about letting people know of our good fortune. She didn't want us to show off in any way. She would say it was better if people didn't know. She would chastise my father, a contractor, if he bragged about his many jobs or a new piece of property he was working on. Over time, I realized the jealousy of others wasn't the only way misfortune could arise, but the jealousy about someone else's good fortune within me could affect my health and well-being. I immediately restructured those thoughts into thoughts of joy and happiness for the good fortune of others.

If you have a tendency towards being secretly jealous of someone else's good fortune, hold tightly to your tiger's eye and use it to help you figure out what you can do in your life to create similar health, wealth, joy, happiness, and relationships, instead of wasting your time being jealous. Raise your self-esteem and take action to create your life as you wish it to be! Golden brown tiger's eye is an excellent stone for improving your self-esteem, mental clarity, and creativity.

Golden Brown Tiger's Eye Affirmation: I am safe. I have constant protection surrounding me, deflecting anything not intended for my highest good. I am grateful to have the courage and self-confidence to create my world.

Essential Oils for the Solar Plexus Chakra

The solar plexus is the part of your consciousness that processes all life has to offer. It is the area where the majority of digestion takes place, so it relates to how you absorb and process food as well as how you deal with your reality. This sunny yellow chakra holds the vibration of joy and optimism or despair and pessimism—the choice is yours.

Your personal power is held at the solar plexus, along with your self-confidence or lack thereof. The following oils can be used as additional tools to bring the sense of smell into your transformational process.

Anise

Anise is commonly used in Italian households—or at least it was in mine. Anisette liquor is often offered to sip with espresso and a twist of lemon rind after a meal. The name "anise" is commonly applied to fennel. While they aren't identical, their uses are similar. Anise oil aids in the integration of thoughts, feelings, and emotions as they affect the solar plexus and your self esteem. Remember, apply oil diluted in a carrier oil to the soles of your feet for effective, safe delivery and remember to use in moderation. Please don't overdo oil application—these oils have real chemical components.

Bergamot

Bergamot is made from the fruit of the Italian citrus tree. It is an antiseptic, antibiotic, antispasmodic, and antidepressant. It is therefore used for depression, stress, tension, fear, hysteria, emotional crisis, and all types of infections. It's the distinctive flavor in Earl Grey tea and is commonly used in perfumery and cosmetics.

Fennel

Oils that are generally good for digestion are fennel, anise, and chamomile. When I was growing up, fennel was commonly used in my household. Mom always added fennel seeds to the tomato sauce served with pasta and of course, I make my sauce the same way. As a vegetable, fennel has the texture of celery and is also beneficial for digestion. Italians often eat fennel before or after a meal, either with antipasto or with salad after a meal. Fennel oil diluted in a carrier oil applied to the soles of your feet will aid in the removal of toxins, flatulence, nausea, and obesity.

Lemon

Lemon oil comes from its fresh fruit peel. It is antibiotic, antiseptic, and a natural insecticide. It's also known for helping to bring mental clarity. I once read a story about how the scent of lemon is used in banks in China to reduce worker error. Historically, lemon has been used to prevent and cure scurvy. Lemon has an overall cleansing action on the body and creates a more alkaline condition considered to be beneficial. Lemon juice in water helps to cleanse the liver over time. (**CAUTION: NEVER ORALLY INGEST THE ESSENTIAL OIL OF LEMON OR ANY OTHER ESSENTIAL OIL.**)

I've used lemon essential oil in a blend for someone who was suffering from pain due to shingles. It helps invigorate the immune system and aids in fighting infectious disease. It is also an antidepressant. The yellow vibration of lemon raises joy and the sense of well-being.

———————

Use the stones, oils, and concepts listed here to restore self-confidence. Release underlying patterns and find the empowered part of you. Remember that it is safe to be powerful in a loving way. Which gemstones and essential oils have you determined will be best to assist you at this moment in your life? Pick a stone and use an oil to maintain an intention to raise your self-esteem and know you are magnificent! Now that you've read about the solar plexus chakra, digest it, joyfully go forth, and shine your light!

five

GREEN AND PINK ENERGY AND THE HEART CHAKRA

*Y*ou are love. Your true essence is love. Be aware that you are love in all you do, say, think, feel, smell, taste, or know, and you will be happy and healthy all the days of your life.

The heart is the bridge between your lower three chakras and your upper three chakras. It is the place of the "I Am" presence, the Christ consciousness, and the Buddha consciousness. The heart center connects us with kindness, love, compassion, tolerance, patience, understanding, and who we truly are. It is a vibration of love in alignment with goodness and gratitude. A person with a balanced heart center is someone who is friendly, compassionate, empathetic, and nurturing.

The green and pink energy of the heart chakra is located in the center of your chest. The primary color is green. The vibration of pink at the heart is the blended energy of red from the root chakra and white from the crown chakra. There is no complementary color per se—the colors are simply green and pink.

The Heart Chakra

Primary Colors: Green, pink

Complementary Colors: Green, pink

Stones: Agate, apophyllite, aventurine, calcite, chrysoprase, goldstone, kunzite, malachite, rhodochrosite, rose quartz, ruby, unakite, watermelon tourmaline, and all pink and/or green stones

Location: The center of your chest

Musical Note: F#

Essential Oils: Jasmine, lavender, neroli, rose

Keywords: Compassion, kindness, love, relationships, and "As above, so below"

Physical Body: Heart, immune system, lungs, lymph and thymus glands

A person with a balanced heart center sees the good in all things. Combined with a balanced solar plexus, you will see the glass half full and the silver lining in every cloud, even amidst adversity. The heart chakra is the place of empathy. An empathetic person can relate to or feel what others feel. When you act from your heart, you feel compassion and have true understanding and tolerance. If the heart chakra is imbalanced, you might smother or over-nurture others. On the other hand, if you are empathetic to the degree that you ignore your own needs, your own heart may suffer.

As you get a deeper understanding of each chakra, you gain a deeper understanding of people and their challenges, as well as your own. This deeper look into each aspect of human nature offers you the opportunity to stop judging yourself and others. As you open your heart, you can allow judgment to turn into simple observation. Just observe any situation, whatever it is, and step away from anything not in alignment with your personal truth.

The Prayer of St. Francis of Assisi sums up the heart center energy. I also recommend that the deeper meaning of this prayer be integrated and intended in all aspects of your life. Post this prayer somewhere and read it often.

Prayer of St. Francis of Assisi
Lord, make me an instrument of your peace,
Where there is hatred, let me sow love;
where there is injury, pardon;
where there is doubt, faith;
where there is despair, hope;
where there is darkness, light;
where there is sadness, joy;
O Divine Master, grant that I may not so much seek to be con-
*   soled as to console;*
to be understood as to understand;
to be loved as to love.
For it is in giving that we receive;
it is in pardoning that we are pardoned;
and it is in dying that we are born to eternal life.

CHARACTERISTICS OF THE HEART CHAKRA

We are in relationship with everything. Relationship is part of our lives down to the minutiae! Obviously, we are in relationship with people, but less obvious is the relationship we have with ourselves.

Our connection with other people has myriad levels, including friendship, neighbors, acquaintances, coworkers, employees, supervisors, authority figures, family, extended family, and so on. Additionally, relationship exists between us and animals, nature in all its forms, and inanimate objects, such as cars, computers, TVs, sofas, recliners, beds, and more. The less obvious connection with ourselves has just as many layers, but it takes conscious intention to uncover awareness of the love we have for ourselves. And within all our connections there are emotions, reactions, and feelings, as well as unconditional love.

All relationship connections come from the heart, the center of ourselves. This is the area in our "beingness" where a bridge exists. This bridge provides the connection from the lower three chakras of earth-centered connection to the upper three chakras of heaven-centered connection. It is the bridge connecting heaven and earth within our own consciousness. The heart center is love—pure love.

Relationships

The heart chakra is the place where you hold the energy of divine love, friendship, romance, and love in every definition of the word. It is the place where you deal with how you behave in any relationship. At all times, you are in a relationship with two parties: yourself and everyone else. Explore ways to optimize both of these relationships and learn how to create the most favorable set of circumstances to attract positive, nurturing, loving individuals into your life.

Though you are in relationship with everything and everyone, your most sacred relationship is the one you have with yourself. Check in with yourself and ask:

> *How is my relationship with myself?*
> *In what tone do I talk to myself?*
> *Do I love myself?*
> *Do I say nice things to myself?*
> *When was the last time I complimented myself?*
> *Do I feel that I look good?*
> *Do I think I'm smart?*

Observing the "mirrors" of how others interact with you will provide your answers. Your coworkers, supervisors, spouse, significant other, family, friends, children, and a variety of people will provide this reflection. Want to know what you need to learn? Look at the people around you, ask yourself what they need to learn, and *then* realize you are looking into a mirror. Your relationships are gifts—lovingly use and appreciate them.

To balance your heart center, get to know yourself better, honor yourself more fully, and spend enjoyable quality time with yourself. You will become a better and more honest friend, partner, and lover because you know who you are. So often, people lose the sense of who they are and what they want when in relationships with others. In order to regain confidence, you must first have a strong sense of yourself.

Feelings and Emotions

The pink and green energy of your heart asks you to come to terms with your feelings and emotions. Feelings and emotions vibrate throughout the emotional body. They are primarily managed by all the chakras. In his DVD *The Science of Miracles*, Gregg Braden explains the difference between feelings and emotions. Although the terms are often used interchangeably, there's a distinct difference:

> Thought gives focus to the emotions—the result is a feeling, if it is heart centered rather than just an emotional reaction. The heart-centered language opens the door to possibilities which are actualized by the energy field or consciousness web or net that underlies everything in the universe. Thought can direct feelings but the *feeling* is the prayer and the strength of that feeling is what creates its

power. External effects create emotions, but they need to be channelled to create positive feelings.

Feelings are a part of our human consciousness, the result of emotions, sentiments, and desires. They are an emotional state you experience. Feelings also include awareness, impressions, and intuition. They give us the capacity to experience higher emotions, such as sensitivity and sensibility. Put another way, feelings are manifestations of emotions.

Emotions are mental states that arise spontaneously without conscious effort. Likewise, feeling (experiencing) emotions (e.g., joy, sorrow, love, and dislike) may also arise without any conscious effort. All of a sudden—voilà!—an emotion you never saw coming bubbles up from within, surprising you and everyone around you.

Loss is a big reason for the rising of emotions. Whether it is the loss of your beloved, a family member, pet, friend, coworker, habit, or material object of value, a void now exists where something real once existed.

Reactions

Unfortunately, when we experience loss, we may blow up at unexpected moments. A blowup may manifest as uncontrollable crying at an inappropriate time, or screaming or acting inappropriately at someone who has stepped over the line. Such a reaction may be way out of proportion and have absolutely nothing to do with the situation at hand.

Blowups are usually embarrassing, hurtful, and uncomfortable for everyone involved. Once the dust settles and everyone takes a deep breath, it's time to sit down and have a nice big piece of humble pie with a large side serving of self-observation. If you ignore the side dish, the level of emotional indigestion or distress may become immeasurable. Have compassion for yourself.

An apology to the recipient of the reaction is vital in order to move forward. It is imperative for you to forgive yourself for your shortcomings. You can't expect anyone else to forgive you if you haven't forgiven yourself. Make a commitment to yourself to delve deep into the underlying emotion that created the blowup. When a blowup or breakdown occurs, it is a huge, blaring sign that you need to pay attention to something you've ignored.

You need to forgive yourself and move into gratitude. Forgiveness happens when you can thank yourself or another "for-giving" you the experience to learn and grow into a better person.

Sage Advice

A sage is someone who is respected for his or her experience, wisdom, and judgment. I consider myself lucky enough to have received sage advice from two very wise men about eruptions and the ensuing emotions those eruptions often cause.

I received the first insight in Miami in September of 2004 while attending a public lecture given by His Holiness the Dalai Lama on world peace and freeing the mind from suffering. In his opening remarks, His Holiness told everyone how he is a simple monk and very human, and that sometimes he gets angry with his staff, who lovingly care for him. He further explained that destructive tendencies like anger, jealousy, and fear can only be eliminated by the strong desire to free ourselves and *all* beings from suffering. This is known as *bodhicitta,* the awakening of the compassionate mind. In order for the world to be in peace, *we*, as individuals, must first and foremost be in peace. We need to develop and sustain peaceful relations with those who are closest to us, our family, friends, coworkers, and neighbors. This, in turn, creates the foundation for peace in the community, the state, the nation, and the world at large. From this story, the Dalai Lama taught me that the key to inner peace is mindfulness.

We need to reflect upon the negativity that we engage in, as this is the cause of our suffering and the suffering of others. We should develop a deep sense of resolve; that from now on, we will not engage in negative thoughts or actions. With this resolve, we declare and purify ourselves. We can rejoice in our own virtuous activities, as well as the virtuous activities of others. We must also develop a deep sense of admiration for the great deeds of historical sages and masters who perfected these skills before us, as they are the great ones who showed us the way.

I also received wise advice from my dad, whom some affectionately and respectfully refer to as the Daddy Lama or Papa Bear. I went to Dad and asked him about how to deal with an out-of-proportion reaction I had to a situation with a client. He shared that it's not easy to learn the ability to control the emotions, but we must keep trying. He said for some of us, it takes a long time—a very long time—but we must continue to try to balance this human quality. I am grateful for his wise and simple advice.

Christ Consciousness and Buddha Consciousness

The heart chakra is the epitome of Christ consciousness and Buddha consciousness. It brings to mind the energy of a bodhisattva. In Tibetan Buddhism, a bodhisattva is someone who is motivated by pure compassion and wisdom. The bodhisattva seeks enlightenment, not only for him- or herself, but for all beings. Those who seek this enlightenment for others as well as themselves are often willing to suffer in order to achieve the goal. Jesus the Christ was a true bodhisattva.

In Buddhism there is the practice of the Four Immeasurables. They are:

May all sentient beings have happiness and its causes.
May all sentient beings be free of suffering and its causes.

May all sentient beings not be separated from sorrowless bliss.
May all sentient beings abide in equanimity, free of bias, attach-
ment, and anger.

Be gentle with yourself and with others. You have no idea what is going on in other people's lives and why they may talk and act as they do. Don Miguel Ruiz's *Four Agreements* (Amber-Allen, 1997) states: "Do not take anything personally. Don't assume anything. Always do your best. Be impeccable with your word." Integrate this teaching into your consciousness. Pay attention to the signs through your reactions or the other feelings your body experiences. Often, the signals are screaming at you! They are trying to tell you to stop, relax, take time to just be, and nurture yourself.

Exercise

LIVING AND LOVING UNCONDITIONALLY

Mute the incessant chatter of your mind and your busy life long enough to recognize feelings that need to be acknowledged. Turn off the TV, step away from the computer, turn off your cell phone, and STOP! Stop, sit, and be still. Focus on your breath and let it all be.

Ask yourself:

Do I allow myself to truly feel my feelings?
Am I burying feelings with busyness?
Do I ignore the feelings that come up?
How do I deal with feelings within me?
Do I live and let live?
Am I quick to point fingers at others and their lifestyles or behav-
iors?

Am I trying to get others to conform to what I believe to be the right way—my way?

Become more familiar with your own feelings and move toward self-acceptance. In turn, it will help you to shift into unconditional love and simple observation of others. Reflect on unconditional loving and unconditional living. Take time to write in your journal.

———

You are in a constant state of growth and change from the moment you are born until the moment you die. In fact, growth and change continue on as you travel into other realms of consciousness and other dimensions when you leave this planet.

When you were a child, your parents loved you unconditionally. As you have grown, changed, and made mistakes (and hopefully learned from those mistakes), you're still blessed with unconditional love. Some of you have had experiences that make it appear as if you have lost unconditional acceptance from your parents. You may have found you have had to unconditionally love yourself as you grew into an adult because of this perception. Your parents still love you; it just feels conditional. While this is a broad statement, I believe it is true in most cases. Hopefully, you were blessed with parents who continue to unconditionally love you as you find your way through adulthood.

As an adult, you must learn to love yourself unconditionally. If you can't do that for yourself, how can you expect anyone else to love you unconditionally? Fortunately, once you learn to love yourself unconditionally, it's easier to love others unconditionally. Of course, this all depends on how conscious you are as you walk through life. Sometimes you can be self-focused and miss what's going on around you. Other times you're so focused on everyone else's business, you miss your own issues and areas for self-improvement!

Living and loving unconditionally are very similar. When you truly love someone, you don't withhold your love because they fail to behave in the manner you want or that society dictates. It may be that the way they express love is simply different from the way you express love.

When I am challenged like this, I read excerpts from *The Writings of Florence Scovel Shinn* (DeVorss & Company, 2003), such as "Real love is selfless and free from fear. It pours itself out upon the object of its affection, without demanding any return. It is joy in the joy of giving. Love is God in Manifestation and the strongest magnetic force in the Universe!" I find that when I read this again and again (or other equally true words), it helps me tremendously, especially when I'm challenged by another's behavior which doesn't meet my expectations. The reminder calms me, aligns me with real love, and helps me release expectations. Remain focused on real love. We'll all be better off because of it!

Sacred Relationship

The heart chakra is the place where you can deepen your relationships. Over many years of ups and downs, strong levels of trust and integrity develop based on history and experience. A foundation is formed because of the time you have invested in your relationships. In healthy relationships, people love and respect each other. Mutual love and respect provide a safe space to overcome personal fears of confrontation. You're able to speak the truth because the relationship is worth overcoming the paralysis of taking action; the relationship can then be preserved. The love is profound enough to enable you to move beyond selfish, self-focused behavior. Such love allows you to act in accordance with what is best to maintain and grow the relationship.

Be aware of others' feelings. Act with true consideration and kindness. Act and think as "we" instead of just "me." Do whatever it takes to preserve the love developed over time. It's much better to speak the truth with love and compassion than to leave things unsaid, hidden, or secretive because you don't have the courage to let another person know how you feel. In relationships, you mirror things back and forth, so you can grow. If one person in the relationship stops participating by not speaking or communicating in some way, the relationship's health and very existence is threatened.

There are also times when it is best to say and do nothing for a while to allow time and space for healing, clarity, and confidence to be restored. This is when you practice the fine art of knowing when retreat is more powerful than action. When you find yourself not knowing what to do, sometimes it's best to do nothing and wait for inspiration and clarity. Be careful, though. Don't wait forever. Timing is everything. Listen to your inner guidance so it won't become a case of too little, too late.

It's important to speak your truth. When we don't speak up, things often become much worse. The level of trust in a relationship diminishes when you act secretly, withhold your feelings, stop communicating, and withdraw for too long. It takes two to tango, right? Both parties need to show up and be present. Relationships are truly a fine art—it takes discernment and finesse to find the balance of honoring yourself while simultaneously honoring how your actions (or lack of action) may affect others.

Conscious Relationship

As we develop spiritually, we enter into relationships with conscious awareness. Conscious awareness means looking at ourselves from many perspectives and authentically being present in our relationships. The variety of past good and bad relationships can lead us to require great courage to move beyond hurt or fear of failure and consciously move into relationship.

Fear is the absence of love. In order to move out of fear, we have to practice opening the heart and allowing love to flow. It helps to be aware that we are *practicing* opening the heart; it takes off a bit of the pressure. The place to start practicing is within the self. Feel and be the love you are. Allow your light to shine fully and you'll find the courage and support necessary for loving relationship experiences.

Allow yourself the gift of loving yourself enough to move forward into intimacy. Even the word "intimacy" sends the heartbeat racing for some. Show up more fully in life and be daring enough to reveal yourself. Intimacy is simply a way to truly know yourself better and love yourself more deeply. If you think about it, intimacy is really a relationship you have with yourself. As you observe yourself, you'll see intimacy is really "into me see." So the question really is "Can you trust yourself?" By trusting yourself, you open up your sacred heart.

Body Parts Related to the Heart Chakra

The areas of the physical body related to the heart chakra are the heart, lungs, immune system, and thymus and lymph glands. Lung challenges, whether pneumonia, asthma, or another severe ailment, usually appears in the midst of grief or loss. The grief over the physical death of a loved one and the loss of a relationship can bring on illnesses related to the lungs.

The heart chakra becomes unbalanced when you don't receive enough attention, appreciation, and love. Use pink and green to amplify the vibration of love and imagine all your cells, bones, and muscles vibrating at this level. I don't use opposite colors or complementary colors at this center—only the pink and green.

Balancing the Heart Chakra

Below is a list of states of being and consciousness that correspond with the gemstones you can use to assist in balancing your heart center and the pink and green vibration in your aura. If you are feeling unloved or unlovable, be sure to add plenty of pink and green vibes into your sacred space. If you're feeling possessive, surround yourself with pink to realign yourself.

Fear of Abandonment

The fear of being abandoned by family or friends comes from experience and a fear of being excluded or rejected stems from past incidents. Use watermelon tourmaline or ruby zoisite to establish love for yourself and recognition that such occurrences were part of the past, not the present moment. This will assist in a return to love. Do whatever it takes to make yourself feel secure. Surround yourself with friends who want to pay attention to you.

Criticism

Peridot, malachite, and chrysoprase can assist in realigning criticism of onself and others. These stones are varying shades of green to heal the bitter energy that has accumulated between the heart and the solar plexus. Find ways to be encouraged and take the time for self-appreciation.

Demanding Behavior

When you or those around you are demanding, try not to judge the behavior. Realize that these are actually screams for love and at-

Agate, Blue Lace

Agate, Brown

Agate, Green

Agate, Pink

Agate, Purple

Amazonite

Amber

Amethyst

Amethyst, Cluster

Angelite

Apatite

Apophyllite, Green

Apophyllite

Aquamarine

Aventurine, Green

Bloodstone

Calcite, Blue

Calcite, Yellow

Calcite, Green

Calcite, Orange   Calcite, Pink

Carnelian   Chrysocolla   Chrysocolla

Chrysoprase   Citrine, Cluster   Citrine, Point

Garnet

Goldstone, Blue

Goldstone, Green

Goldstone, Orange

Hematite

Jasper, Dalmatian

Jasper, Red

Jasper, Yellow

Kunzite

Kyanite

Lapis Lazuli

Lepidolite

Malachite

Moonstone

Obsidian, Black

Obsidian, Golden Sheen

Obsidian, Rainbow

Obsidian, Snowflake

Peridot

Quartz, Cathedral

Quartz,
Channeling

Quartz, Double Terminated

Quartz, Clear

Quartz, Elestial

Quartz,
Herkimer Diamond

Quartz, Isis

Quartz,
Laser Wand

Quartz,
Phantom

Quartz,
Record Keeper

Quartz, Relationship

Quartz, Rose

Quartz, Self Healed

Quartz, Tabular Faden

Quartz, Time Link

Quartz,
Single Terminated

Quartz,
Vogel Cut

Quartz,
Window

Rhodochrosite

Ruby

Selenite

Sodalite

Tigers Eye, Blue

Tigers Eye, Golden Brown

Tigers Eye, Red

Tourmaline, Black

Tourmaline, Watermelon

Turquoise

Unakite

tention. While being demanding is uncomfortable or disconcerting, it is likely a result of learned behavior. Amplify the energy of love by holding kunzite and pink tourmaline. Remember, there is plenty of love everywhere, starting from within yourself.

Possessiveness

The strong yet gentle vibrations of pink tourmaline, kunzite, and rose quartz will open the heart to recognize the truth of love's abundance. Love is available in unlimited supply. As the heart opens to love with consciousness, the need for possessiveness dissipates.

GEMSTONES FOR THE HEART CHAKRA

Positive affirmations for each gemstone are included below. These affirmations are suggestions to focus on while using the stones for balancing your heart chakra. Remember, the stones are tools that will help you amplify your intention and maintain focus.

Agate

This gemstone comes in many colors. Many of the brighter agate stones like the bright green, hot pink, dark blue, and vibrant purple are dyed. These dyes in no way detract from the good vibes of the stones. Dyed agate stones are happy stones, and most children (as well as many adults) are drawn to them. Agate stones also come in multicolored slices. Slices are pretty to place in a stand on a windowsill; let the light shine through them to illuminate the good vibrations. Both green and agate open your heart.

Green or Pink Agate Affirmation: I allow love. My heart is open.

Apophyllite

Sea-foam green clusters of apophyllite are tools for awakening the heart chakra without fear of repeating past patterns of hurt. Apophyllite is gentle yet extremely effective. It is powerful in bringing the vibration of love to relax and open the heart chakra muscles. Once this chakra opens, the free flow of love provides avenues for healing on all levels.

Apophyllite Affirmation: I am connected with the Divine. My heart is open. I give and receive love fully and easily. I am secure in the love I have for myself.

Calcite

Pink and green calcite supports you during a change of heart. It is very nurturing for your heart center during a relationship change such as divorce, marriage, or any nonromantic endeavor, including a professional relationship. Green dogtooth calcite has a mossy look, and I have found that the soft color combined with the pointed crystalline structure activates "getting to the source of the healing challenge" energy to heal the problem once and for all. This stone holds a vibration that reminds me of the healing properties of herbs. Optical calcite typically occurs in pale green and pale pink shades, and I've found it beneficial for gaining clarity in affairs of the heart.

Pink or Green Calcite Affirmation: I feel nurtured by my friends and family. I am blessed with nurturing vibrations wherever I go! I am gentle. All change brings more love and better life situations.

Chrysoprase

This stone's soothing green semi-opaque color brings peace and calm to your heart. It is a heart chakra stone and provides a peace similar to ocean waves gently lapping at the shore. A member of the chalcedony family, chrysoprase is an apple green or a sea-foam green color.

The soothing energy of chrysoprase's green shades are comforting in times of heartbreak. Using this stone is like a healing salve on a sore while being gently rocked in the arms of a dear one to help make it feel "all better." Since being introduced to chrysoprase, I've wanted a bathtub made from it—I think it would be deliciously calming and nurturing to sit in a bathtub made from chrysoprase. I can even imagine the translucency of the stone as light filters through the water. Perhaps I had a tub like that in an earlier Atlantis lifetime. A girl can dream, right?

Chrysoprase Affirmation: All is well. Everything is okay. My heart is open and I allow love. I am nurtured. I am nurturing.

Goldstone (Green)

Goldstone is actually a man-made stone and really isn't a true mineral; it's glass made from copper and copper salts. Despite its nature, the fact remains that goldstone amplifies intention when used with conscious direction. Green goldstone activates your heart chakra and opens it to give and receive love.

Green Goldstone Affirmation: I open my heart and shine the love that I am to everyone I meet. I have plenty of money. I am blessed with the greatest family and wonderful friends.

Green Aventurine

When all is well in your world, you feel like the luckiest person alive! This green stone is the four-leaf clover of the gemstone kingdom. It carries the vibration of good luck and good fortune. It's great for travel, and you can use it with conscious intention to have a fun, safe, smooth journey. Most importantly, this gemstone's earthy green vibration provides healing of the heart on all levels. The healing energy is for the physical heart, of course, but it certainly aids in healing relationships as well.

Likewise, employ green aventurine to bring more prosperity— green cash! When combined with citrine, it's known as the "merchant stone combination." Keep it in your cash drawer if you have a cash register or wherever you keep you money, such as a wallet, pocket, piggy bank—or secret hiding place.

Green Aventurine Affirmation: I am very grateful for all my good luck. I am so lucky. It's so easy for me to be prosperous and have plenty of money. All my travels are easy and effortless. Travel experiences are flowing, fun, and safe.

Kunzite

The pink variety of this stone is one of love. Kunzite also occurs in green, violet, and white varieties. This mineral emanates a loving vibration that radiates in a wide radius. Kunzite reminds you how to love and be loved. Once the memory is stimulated, you can consciously manifest more loving people around you.

Kunzite is a good stone for relationships. Use it to gain clarity about what you do and don't want in a relationship. Many people seem to struggle with their love lives, and kunzite can assist in bringing forth mindfulness to help us define how we want to be loved. When you find yourself confused about any relationship you're in, ask yourself these simple questions: *Does my partner love me the way I want and deserve to be loved? Does my partner allow me to love him/her the way I want to love?*

Kunzite Affirmation: There is a huge bubble of love shining brightly around me. I live within a dome of love, light, and well-being. I attract loving friends and family who support and honor me. I am filled with gratitude and love. I am love, and all that surrounds and is attracted to me is love.

Malachite

The swirling shades of green in malachite help to move the energy in your heart. The swirls create concentric circles that appear like bull's-eyes throughout the stone. This connects you to the ability to get to the heart of the issue using its focus. If there are issues to be addressed and you believe it's time to address them, use malachite to aim your sights on uncovering and healing them.

Malachite Affirmation: I easily get to the heart of any matter at hand. My heart is focused on love, light, and well-being. Even when things appear to swirl around me, I am able to stay focused on loving myself and others.

Rhodochrosite

This peachy pink to rosy red stone brings energy from the heart to the navel, creating a bridge between the two chakra centers. The challenges and buried emotions stored within the navel need love. It is really quite simple, when you think about it: the key to restoring balance is to instill more love where there is pain, heartache, or angst. Rhodochrosite provides a bridge to love.

Rhodochrosite is one of the primary stones used for rebalancing and rejuvenating the cells during and after cancer treatment. It sends nurturance to the cells by instilling love. The love envelopes every bone, muscle, and cell with love. It regenerates cells in a healthy, balanced form using visualization.

Rhodochrosite has a high silver content, and some of the best specimens have been found in Colorado. As such, it has been adopted as their state stone. I visited the silver mines of Silverton, Colorado, on a trip on the Durango-Silverton Narrow Gauge Railroad. The miners often would cast away the rhodochrosite in pursuit of silver. The rhodochrosite was discarded due to the stone's manganese content, a destructive mineral to silversmithing.

Now, however, gemstone collectors find the rhodochrosite specimens valuable.

Rhodochrosite Affirmation: I am love. I am balanced. My cells regenerate and rejuvenate in a healthy way.

Rose Quartz

The pastel pink vibration of rose quartz elicits love, comfort, compassion, tolerance, acceptance, nurturance, and well-being. This stone is the stone of gentle love, which can be compared to the nurturing, safe, unconditional love of a mother. It is the epitome of the heart chakra. Use rose quartz to help you heal from loss—loss of love, a friend or pet, or in any sense. It nurtures you and supports you while you grieve.

Rose quartz manages feelings of anger and anxiety by softening your vibration and filling you with love. Rose quartz is a good stone for children. It's helpful for keeping away temper tantrums; however, I wouldn't recommend giving the child a piece of it while they are in the midst of their tantrum, as you may end up dodging flying rocks!

Larger pieces of tumbled rose quartz added to a bath offer a soothing solution for a stress-filled day. It regenerates your cells, bones, and muscles, and calms your spirit. Add it to your bedroom to bring peaceful sleep filled with loving vibrations.

Rose Quartz Affirmation: I am love. My life is filled with love, light, and well-being. My skin and cells are healthy and rejuvenate daily. I am gentle and nurturing, and I surround myself with people who are also gentle and nurturing.

Unakite

This pink and green stone is good for the heart and navel chakras. It opens the heart and balances emotions. It is generally considered to be a balancing stone due to its nearly equal amounts of peachy pink and green colors. It is helpful during mood swings.

Do you have a tendency to judge yourself or judge others in a mood swing? This is the most important time to have understanding and compassion for others and for yourself. Use unakite when you want to shift from judgment to observation—there's a huge difference between the two.

Unakite Affirmation: I am safe. All is well. Only goodness and joy are allowed in my energy field. I have compassionate understanding for myself and others. I am able to observe situations and am grateful for having a nonjudgmental perspective.

Watermelon Tourmaline

Tourmaline comes in many colors—black, brown, pink, blue, green, teal, and yellow. Some tourmaline stones are multicolored. When there are two colors, it's called bicolor tourmaline. Dark pink tourmaline, also known as rubellite, often occurs with green tourmaline, one on top of the other. The combination of colors in tourmaline determines the appropriate use of the stone with a specific chakra. The occurrence of the colors in watermelon tourmaline is displayed one inside the other, typically with the pink in the center of the piece and the green on the outer layer of the stone, just like its namesake fruit.

Watermelon tourmaline aids in staying focused on your heart and the love that you are. It exemplifies all the qualities of the heart chakra.

Watermelon Tourmaline Affirmation: All I do comes from my heart. I think with my heart, speak through my heart, and act from my heart. I know my core is love.

ESSENTIAL OILS FOR THE HEART CHAKRA

When all is said and done, it's all about love. Love is all there is. Where does the love come from? I know it sounds cliché, but healing and realignment for everyone is all about opening the heart. Here are some aromas that will open your heart and bring in those love vibrations.

Jasmine

Jasmine oil activates the heart and moves the energy toward love. It is expensive—flowers from which the oil is derived must be picked by hand before sunrise on the first day the blossoms open. This oil requires a thousand pounds of flowers for sixteen ounces of oil. It is a very important ingredient for the perfume industry, and as you know, supply and demand determine price.

Jasmine is used as an aphrodisiac and for fertility. It also calms stress-related conditions and helps relieve depression. This oil may be used for the heart, solar plexus, and navel chakras.

While inhaling the scent of jasmine, visualize a romantic relationship as you wish it to be. Hold a rose quartz or wear it while wearing jasmine oil. Watch how your thoughts, intentions, scent, and colored gemstone attract your heart's desire into reality!

Jasmine will also connect you with your sacred heart. Allow the aroma to raise you to heightened states of spiritual awareness and become one with the Divine.

Lavender

Lavender oil, addressed in the third eye chakra section in chapter 7, calms and assuages heartache, and aligns you with the vibration of gentle nurturing.

Neroli

Neroli comes from the flowers of Italian orange trees and is the vibration of sweetness and the nectar of love. Neroli assists you in the activation of joy and happiness in your heart. This oil calms your nervous energy and allows you to experience euphoria. It is a calmative as well as an aphrodisiac.

Rose

Roses are most often associated with love and romance. Roses are given as a token of love, and its oil is also known to bring forth an open heart. True rose essential oil is very expensive—if it's not expensive, it's not true rose oil. It takes about 10,000 pounds of flowers to make sixteen ounces of rose oil, or 60,000 rose petals to make a single ounce!

Rose oil offers you the opportunity to expand your heart chakra and connect with your inner and outer beauty. Rose helps you love yourself. As you love yourself fully and completely, your world will reflect the same back to you. Rose oil is good for the heart chakra and brings more love into your sex life.

———————

When the heart chakra is imbalanced, you may observe yourself or someone else being demanding, moody, overly critical, possessive, or showing a tendency to control others. These kinds of behavior indicate that the heart center needs more love. Feelings of abandonment and fear of injury can close the heart. By contrast, a balanced heart center is demonstrated through compassion, empathy, and a friendly attitude. A person who can see the good in things and is nurturing in a healthy way has an open heart.

six

Pastel Blue Energy
and the
Throat Chakra

*T*he pastel blue energy of the throat chakra extends in a band of energy around the neck. It encompasses the area around the ears, nose, and mouth. The energy is blue, like the color of the sky and the turquoise stone. This chakra enhances communication, both on a physical and celestial level. The throat chakra is the place to connect with divine timing, angels, and invisible guides.

The primary color associated with the throat is pastel blue, yet it also holds the vibration of all shades of blue, including the blue-green colors in shades of turquoise, amazonite, and apatite.

The Throat Chakra

Primary Colors: Dark blue, sky blue, turquoise

Complementary Colors: Red, although it is rarely used in this area

Stones: Amazonite, angelite, aquamarine, blue calcite, blue lace agate, turquoise

Other Stones for Balance: Lapis lazuli, sodalite
Location: Throat and neck area
Musical Note: A
Essential Oils: "Auntie M's Anti," eucalyptus, lemongrass, tea tree
Keywords: Communication, creative expression, divine timing, truth
Physical Body: Ears, eyes, muscles, nerves, throat, thyroid

CHARACTERISTICS OF THE THROAT CHAKRA

The energy center at the throat and neck area is a portal to the connection with the Divine and unseen realms of consciousness. While its earthly role is primarily related to our ability to communicate, express, and listen to others, its function is much more mystical and esoteric. Most communication is perceived as auditory and visual. Yet there is another largely unexplainable level—the plane where information is received from otherworldly beings, such as our loved ones who have passed over, our angels, and our spirit guides. When we follow guidance received, even when it doesn't seem to make immediate sense or it comes from an inexplicable source, coincidence and divine timing can play a role in our lives. Allow divine timing to be a normal part of existence and watch the ease in which life flows!

Communication

The throat chakra is primarily related to communication. Communication is not just the action of speech and expression, but also the ability to truly listen and hear what others say.

How often do you think of something else while someone is speaking to you? I bet you are even thinking of other things while you're reading this. Before someone has finished speaking, do you find yourself thinking of a response? It's very typical to start formulating a response before someone has finished talking, and it becomes extremely obvious when you interrupt or talk over someone speaking in order to make your point.

Active Listening

It's important to learn active listening and to be aligned in the present moment. What this means is that you aren't thinking of fifteen other things or distracted in multitasking activities. To be in the present moment requires the ability to maintain singular focus on the subject at hand.

Do you think before you speak? Do you have a tendency to give unsolicited advice? Have you ever noticed that when you start to share your feelings with someone, they immediately try to fix it or tell you what to do? Such people are not being active listeners. If they were truly listening, they may have realized that all you wanted was for someone to listen compassionately!

Learn to be more sensitive to people and where they may be in any given moment. Make it your intention to open your ears and truly hear. Be present instead of stepping ahead within conversations.

A friend of mine taught me the value of dyading, a process where two people actively listen to each other without interrupting to make the occasional comment as you would in a conversation. Learning this active listening process has assisted me in improving my relationships with others.

Exercise

DYADING

Sit across from the person with whom you will dyad. Together, decide on what issue or situation you want to improve and receive clarity.

One person asks the other person a question. Let's say you need clarity on issues relating to prosperity or relationships. The question to ask is simple: "How do you feel about prosperity?" or "How do you feel about your relationships?"

The one who is speaking goes within for a few moments of reflection, observes the breath, and then allows a flow of thoughts or stream of consciousness to come forth. The speaker expresses this stream of thoughts, feelings, and emotions.

The one listening is doing just that—listening. That's it. Nothing else. No reactions, facial expression, gestures, or sounds. The listener is simply to be present—fully present—without judgment to fully hear what the one speaking is expressing. When the one speaking feels complete, they switch roles. The same process is repeated. Now the listener becomes the speaker, and is allowed the space to communicate without interruption or any reaction from the person listening.

This process of switching from listener to speaker and back again continues until both parties feel they have expressed all that needs to be said. A completed dyading results in a stronger connection of intimacy, understanding, and compassion. It opens a new level of respectful communication between participants and allows for a better relationship.

The feeling of truly being heard and having someone holding a space for you to easily express yourself is amazingly comforting. It also creates an avenue for profound clarity.

Divine Timing

At the throat center, you hold your space of being content and aligned with yourself. This relates to what I mentioned earlier about being truly present in every moment and not thinking about some future point in time. When you're content with yourself and others, you have less need to be thinking of or speaking about the future. Wherever you go, you're at the right place, at the right time! And the more you believe this to be true, the more you *are* exactly where you are supposed to be. This feeling is being in alignment with divine timing.

Divine timing can be created through intention. Use pastel blue gemstones like angelite or blue lace agate while you form the intention to always be at the right place at the right time. Imagine, know, and believe you interact with the right people for the highest good of all. The vibration of being centered and aligned opens you up to being in the right place at the right time.

When you are aligned with the Divine, you are able to lead a charmed life. Life flows smoothly and easily. So how do you go about manifesting that? Start by actually intending that no matter where you go and what you do, you will be at the right place at the right time, as if it were divinely orchestrated by your angels.

Blue is the color of inspiration, and inspiration is sent to you by the angels. Use angelite, celestite, aquamarine, turquoise, or any other pastel blue stones in connection with the thought-form that you intend to lead a charmed life. Believe that you are charmed and aligned with cosmic coincidence, and it will be so.

Coincidence

Contemplate the phenomenon of coincidence. Coincidence happens when two or more events occur simultaneously. To coincide, things must appear in the same place or at the same time. Some believe that coincidence happens by chance, but I have a different view, as do many of my colleagues: coincidence is the result of divine alignment and timing. Divine alignment happens when you are on the correct path, doing what you came to do, being helpful to others while helping yourself.

Invite or invoke coincidence into your life. How? Just state it out loud to yourself or to your angels. State what? "I now invite and invoke divine timing and cosmic coincidence to be a normal, daily occurrence in my life for the highest good of all."

Invisible Helpers

The throat chakra is your connection for communication with your invisible helpers. You have many invisible helpers around you at every moment of your life. It doesn't matter if you are conscious of them or not—they are still there watching over you, inspiring and guiding you through your path in life. These invisible helpers are with you 24/7, whether you are sleeping or awake. When you're ready to be conscious of them, they're only a thought away.

Angels respond to your thought-forms; all it takes to invite them is to form the thought; they respond to our innermost thoughts and feelings. For more details about working with the angelic realm, read the "Going Up? Connection with Higher Realms" exercise in chapter 8. Although all three upper chakras are directly associated with angels, guides, and loved ones on the other side, the throat chakra is the center that allows communication to flow through the senses of hearing, smelling, tasting, and speaking.

Although you most likely think of communication as the spoken or written word, communication encompasses the higher vibration of the creative expression of who you truly are. Another form of spiritual communication is prayer and meditation. Prayer and meditation can assist you in connecting with higher wisdom and all your guides and angels. Silence and physical stillness provide the mental and physical quietude necessary to hear and know the truth.

The throat chakra is the place where the energy of being able to speak your truth, live your truth, and be your truth resides. As the throat chakra becomes more developed and balanced, you'll be able to speak your truth, be your truth, live your truth, and act in truth. Amazonite is a stone of truth and integrity that assists you in expressing the truth in your life.

The throat chakra is the spiritual center of creativity, just as the navel is the physical center of creativity. In some cases, you might find it best to work on the lower chakra when the upper chakra is out of balance, or vice versa. I have found that going directly for the jugular (so to speak) is too aggressive an approach, whereas if you approach the soft underbelly gently, you can relax enough to touch the jugular for deep healing purposes. If a strong gut reaction to a core issue pops up, however, perhaps a nice, soothing conversation would be a better approach to address the issue.

I compare the gentle problem-approaching method to a talented massage therapist. When you have a sore muscle or one that won't stop spasming, a good massage therapist will work the areas surrounding the problematic muscle to release the tension and relax you. Only after some release has taken place can the massage therapist work on the real the soreness or spasm itself without creating more pain.

Blue is a calming color, and is the color of peace, tranquility, inspiration, and spaciousness. Blue is comforting, and is in the cool family of color theory. It is the color of choice to balance any inflammation, including an inflamed state of consciousness, body part, or manner of speaking. The throat center, then, is responsible for communication—creation through the spoken word.

Word Patrol

The words you speak and think create most of your reality. How often do you say the following to yourself?

- *This is killing me.*
- *What a pain in the neck!*
- *You're making me crazy.*
- *I'm such a jerk.*

Well, stop it! I say to all of those negative phrases, "cancel, clear, delete!" By verbalizing "cancel, clear, delete!" to the universe, you are in effect erasing the words and clearing your "screen" to start again. Before you speak, consider what you may be feeling. For example, instead of saying, "This is killing me!" how about "This is upsetting to me," or maybe "My feelings are hurt."

When you become aware of what you're putting "out there" with your words, you create a better, healthier, and more balanced reality for yourself and those around you. Every single statement, word, and thought sends out a vibration that comes back to you. Simple self-observation or word patrol can shift these unconscious patterns with words.

When the throat chakra is out of balance, you may be arrogant, dogmatic, self-righteous, indignant, or excessively talkative or quiet. An out-of-balance throat chakra may also manifest in conditions such as being scared, timid, unreliable, devious, and inconsistent.

Although turquoise or pastel blue is the color for the balanced condition at the throat, I rarely use complementary red-colored stones for the out-of-balance condition. Instead, I choose yellow stones for self-confidence at the solar plexus and red stones at the root to activate the motivation to be more vocal. Pastel blue stones at the throat will help bring any words to the surface.

Body Parts Related to the Throat Chakra

The physical parts of the body directly related to the throat chakra energy system are the ears, nose, and throat, as well as the eyes. Nerves, muscles, and the thyroid are also associated with this center. These systems within the physical body provide the ability to communicate in the world. For example, you hear with your ears, you smell with your nose, and you verbalize with the organs in your throat. The mouth, tongue, and the rest of that physical area of your body are included in this chakra as well. We also express using our eyes, definitely its own form of communication. Similarly, we receive messages using sight. This upper chakra overlaps energetically and systemically with the other two upper chakras of the third eye and the crown (see chapters 7 and 8 respectively).

BALANCING THE THROAT CHAKRA

To restore balance in the throat chakra, use positive thoughts combined with crystals and gemstones to reconnect with your ability to express yourself along with the courage to communicate your truth. Below is a list of challenging states that often accompany an imbalance in the throat chakra. As you use the gemstones and colors, you will experience the change you want to see. Use angelite, amazonite, turquoise, blue lace agate, and other light blue stones to activate your intention.

Communication in General

In order to improve your communication skills, carry any light blue stones you can find. Blue calcite will assist you in making changes in the way you express yourself. Aquamarine will assist you when you are speaking to others, especially in regard to travel. Use blue lace agate, angelite, dumortierite, and celestite for your throat chakra needs.

Communication with Angels and Guides

Angelite and celestite are good for communicating with angels and receiving messages from the spirit realm, including deceased loved ones, guides, and ascended masters.

Honesty

The absolute best stone to use when you need to speak your truth with grace is amazonite. Amazonite is the stone to use when honesty must prevail and justice must be served.

Sense of Divine Timing

The development of divine timing lies solely within your own mind and belief system. Intend and know that you are always at places, with people, and in situations the angelic realm has synchronized. This strong belief aligns you with divine inspiration, which ignites divine right action to make it so. Use angelite, celestite, turquoise, and amazonite while holding the intention that you are always in the right place at the right time.

Gemstones for the Throat Chakra

When working with the upper chakras, I rarely use complementary colors. At the throat chakra, I use all the shades of blue, preferring pastel and turquoise shades. My favorite stones for the throat are angelite and amazonite. They activate honesty, truth, integrity, and divine timing.

Positive affirmations for each gemstone are included below. These affirmations are suggestions for focus while using the stones for balancing your throat chakra. Remember, stones are tools that will help you amplify intention and maintain focus.

Agate

Agate gemstones come in many colors. Pair the color with the corresponding chakra to know its meaning. All agates are grounding, especially brown agate. Blue agates stimulate good communication. Some agates are blue naturally, like blue lace agate, but many blue-colored agates have been dyed. Enjoy all stones, regardless of whether they've been artificially altered a bit—the color is still vibrating. Blue lace agate is helpful to send and receive communication and assistance from the angels and your spirit guides, as well as with your friends, family, and colleagues.

Blue Lace Agate Affirmation: I express myself with ease and grace. I find the right words and have the courage to speak my truth.

Amazonite

Amazonite is the stone of truth and honesty. Carry amazonite when you wish to know the truth about any matter. It provides the courage to speak your truth, know your truth, live your truth, and be your truth. When used with conscious intent, you can use amazonite to attract people into your life who act with honesty and integrity. It also helps you communicate honestly and gracefully. Amazonite is helpful in matters requiring legal assistance in order for the truth to be revealed. Bring amazonite with you into court to maintain focus on the truth.

Customers at The Crystal Garden frequently ask what stone is good for this or that. One day, a customer asked me for a stone to help her boyfriend. He was going to a court hearing, and she wanted to give him a stone to carry in his pocket, as well as one for the attorney representing him. Naturally, I recommended amazonite, as it would help bring the truth to light so justice would be served. But in this case, the customer surprised me and asked,

"What other stones do you have? Because I want to keep him from going to jail—that one won't help him!"

Amazonite Affirmation: I am surrounded by honest people of integrity. I live my truth and speak my truth with ease. I am eloquent and I easily find the words to express myself.

Angelite

This stone of the angels is the perfect stone to bring peace and calm into your life. The calming sky blue color associated with the throat chakra provides the opportunity for peace through clear communication, leading to deeper understanding. Communication involves being a good listener. Use angelite to improve your listening skills. True communication involves accurately hearing what others say.

Angelite aids in manifesting a conscious connection with your angels and spirit guides. Your invisible helpers always answer your prayers and communicate with you whether or not you are consciously aware of it. They provide insight and clues through signs and symbols throughout your day. With conscious intention, angelite can help you become more aware of the messages being sent your way. You will begin to find the answers to your prayers in messages that you see in nature, billboards, magazine and newspaper articles, bumper stickers and more. Animals, birds, and insects that appear on your path often bring significant messages. Look up their meanings in Ted Andrews' many books, such as *Animal Speak, Animal Wise,* and *Nature Speak*. Angels and spirit guides inspire you with a thought or an idea, so it's up to you to take action.

Angelite Affirmation: I am grateful to have all my invisible helpers assist me in my life. I live a charmed life, and am always at the right place at the right time. I am a good listener. I receive guidance and messages from my spirit guides and angels all the time.

Aquamarine

Aquamarine helps you communicate your feelings and emotions with poise and ease. If you feel a block in your emotional body, use this stone consciously to gently wade through feelings hidden beneath the surface. Take some aquamarine into the bath or shower and form the intention to get in touch with the watery nature of your emotions. Make it your intention to become consciously aware of your feelings and any disturbing emotions will dissipate.

The watery nature of aquamarine has connections with the sea, all sea life, and even mermaids. If you are attracted to communicating or swimming with the dolphins, the vibration and sparkly energy of aquamarine can be used to support this pursuit. Aquamarine is a wonderful amulet to give to a seafaring friend for boating, scuba diving, or any seafaring adventure.

Aquamarine Affirmation: I am in touch with my emotions and feelings. It is safe to feel my feelings. I express my feelings with ease and tact. I have safe voyages by sea and air. I am blessed with good communication skills.

Calcite

Calcite occurs in orange, blue, honey, brown, green, pink, red, and clear varieties. It also appears in different forms such as masses or chunks, rhomboid, and dogtooth formation. Blue calcite for the throat chakra can help you change the manner in which you communicate; it will bring forth angelic assistance to guide your communication to be filled with grace and diplomacy.

Blue Calcite Affirmation: I express myself with ease, grace, and diplomacy. I find the words I need easily and in perfect timing to state what needs to be said.

Turquoise

As the name of the stone indicates, turquoise is a blue-green stone. It is relatively soft, and is found in varying qualities, some of which are stabilized to maintain the stone's solidity. Turquoise is beneficial to align the throat chakra to your higher truth. Turquoise helps you connect with the cosmic energies from the sky above. This stone is revered by the Native American people for connection with Father Sky, and is often coupled in jewelry with coral to connect with Mother Earth, bringing heaven and earth together. Use this stone to help you know, speak, and live your truth.

Turquoise Affirmation: I am aligned with my truth. I speak my truth with ease and grace. I am connected with the cosmic energies available that bring me clear guidance.

Essential Oils for the Throat Chakra

The pastel blue energy holds the vibration of communication with self, others, and all your invisible helpers. It calls forth the aid of guides and angels to bring well-being into your life through synchronicity and divine timing. On a physical level, the throat energy must be clear and flow in order to send and receive information. It's like a clearinghouse of sorts, or maybe like a high-speed Internet connection. In a high-speed Internet connection, messages are easily received and sent, whereas with a dial-up connection, messages are frequently not sent or received, or they take too long to get where they're supposed to go, and the opportunity is missed.

Auntie M's Anti

This blend is intended as an anti-fungal, anti-bacterial, anti-septic, anti-biotic, anti-parasitic, and anti-viral tool. Use in on a hankie, cotton ball, or bandana to assist in relieving symptoms of sinus infections, the flu, sore throats, bronchial discomfort, and congestion. This blend helps clear out toxins on all levels. The ingredients, all of which apply to the throat chakra, are lavender, eucalyptus, lemon, tea tree, and clove. All of these oils have anti-infectious, antiparasitic, antibiotic, antifungal, and antiseptic properties. Clearing the sinuses, bronchial system, and all congestion provides the avenue for thinking and expressing clearly.

Eucalyptus

Eucalyptus clears the passageways of the ears, throat, nose, and lungs on the physical level. Energetically, use eucalyptus to connect the throat chakra with your intentions. Imagine it helps you open the channel for communication on all levels—physically, spiritually, mentally, and emotionally.

Eucalyptus clears away the vibes of negative words that have been spoken. It's effective for removing the vibration of verbal and emotionally abusive conversations. The cleansing action also prevents the energy from returning, especially when used with clear intention. This works equally well whether you're the one who has a tendency to speak destructively, as well as when you want to clear away the energy of someone who speaks inappropriately to you.

Lemongrass

Despite its name, lemongrass is not a citrus fruit; it's a lemon-scented perennial grass that grows up to four feet tall. Lemongrass is an antidepressant also useful in treating states of exhaustion. It lifts spirits and gets things moving again. Due to its antiseptic nature, it prevents the spread of contagious diseases, especially upper respiratory infections. Lemongrass can be helpful in relieving some jet lag symptoms. I especially like to use essential oils when I travel. I always carry a number of tightly sealed bottles of oils and use them in hotel rooms that need energetic cleansing, as well as for freshening up.

Tea Tree

Tea tree clears away infections of the throat, mouth, and gums. Tea tree is useful when there is a "fungus among us." It is antifungal, anti-infectious, antibiotic, antiviral, antiparasitic, antiseptic, anti-inflammatory, and much more. At The Crystal Garden, I use it as one of the main ingredients in my Auntie M's Anti blend, perfect for use in airplane travel. I encourage you to make your own blends, but remember to look up each oil to learn about the qualities and contraindications before use.

Tea tree is also good for insect bites, and it's one of the few oils that helps with sea lice and red ant bites—an important fact to know if you live in south Florida. It's also helpful for nail fungus, sore throats, boils, acne, and all infections.

———

Use the pastel blue vibration to connect with your higher truth. Play with the oils and the gemstones to help you remember your truth, to speak your truth and live in your truth. When we find that connection, divine timing and coincidence becomes a normal part of existence. Look up to the blue sky, touch an angelite stone in your pocket, or sniff the scent of eucalyptus as a constant reminder that you are in communication with all levels of consciousness at all times.

seven

INDIGO BLUE ENERGY AND THE THIRD EYE CHAKRA

*D*eep within the seat of your consciousness is a place where all is known. Through meditation, you can awaken your consciousness and access this place whenever you choose.

Indigo blue energy, or the third eye chakra, is located behind the center of your forehead. The primary colors associated with the third eye are indigo, purple, and dark blue. To connect with your third eye, place your attention on the center of your forehead. Move your attention behind that spot and imagine you are taking a walk down a hallway to the center of your brain. If you were to put an imaginary line through the center of the top of your head that vertically intersects with the hallway, this intersection is where you would stop and imagine that you are opening the doorway to your subconscious psychic center. As you develop your third eye, your subconscious and unconscious becomes more conscious.

The third eye center is the place of your intuition and your ability to "see" the unseen, know the unknown, feel the intangible, and connect with the invisible world of Spirit. The third eye is the center for your higher intuition. Intuition is your ability to have direct access to the truth, independent of any type of logical or reasoning process.

THE THIRD EYE CHAKRA

Primary Colors: Dark blue, indigo, purple
Complementary Colors: Red, orange, yellow
Stones: Agate, amethyst, apophyllite, clear quartz, goldstone, lapis lazuli, selenite, sodalite, tiger's eye
Location: Behind the center of your forehead
Musical Note: A
Essential Oils: Frankincense, grapefruit, helichrysum, lavender, peppermint, rosemary, sandalwood
Keywords: Channel, charismatic, egomaniac, intuition, telepathy
Physical Body: Brain, ears, eyes, pineal and pituitary glands

CHARACTERISTICS OF THE THIRD EYE CHAKRA

Everyone is intuitive. Regardless of whether we are conscious of it or not, much of what we do is based on feelings and intuition. The actions we take are often based on the feelings and thoughts of those around us. Imagine if we all became consciously aware of our intuitive abilities and deliberately acted upon our insights to be an instrument of good in our own lives and in the lives of others. What a wonderful world we would live in! Telepathy, the ability to hear or know the thoughts of others, is a key trait of our intuition. We pick up the thoughts of all those around us using the six intuitive senses, which I refer to as the six "clairs" (see more on these later on). It is through the use and awareness of the mental, physical, spiritual, and emotional bodies that information is stored and retrieved and then used as we walk through life. Now, let's become cognitive—aware of the process of acquiring knowledge by the use of reason, intuition, or perception.

INTUITION DEVELOPMENT

Your third eye develops over time, so it's neither necessary nor advisable to try to move your psychic senses along too quickly. Since your mental state is closely connected to your intuitive nature, it is wise to allow development to unfold more naturally. An out-of-balance third eye center may present itself as schizophrenia, a mental illness associated with impairment of the perception and the expression of reality. I have an unproven theory that some cases of schizophrenia may actually have started from psychic impressions and skills gone awry. Stay grounded in reality, and use the protection and grounding techniques provided in this book to maintain a realistic intuition development.

Imbalance in the third eye chakra can also result in oversensitivity, which may then develop into codependency or continued enabling of someone engaging in inappropriate behavior. Be mindful when developing your third eye, because as you gain access to your innate powers of intuition and psychic abilities, you could develop an overinflated ego.

When the third eye is out of balance, you may observe yourself becoming an egomaniac. Then again, if you truly *are* an egomaniac, you probably won't be aware of it! Egomania stems from having developed the psychic senses to such an extent that you think you know everything. Unfortunately, becoming increasingly psychic does not guarantee maturity and humility. Such people may not be spiritually evolved, though they may have increased their intuitive skills. However, many have intellectually integrated the spiritual adept's sage wisdom while remaining a humble person. An authoritarian attitude and lack of social skills are signs of egomania.

I've met many spiritual teachers over the years whose third eyes were well developed. While the majority of these teachers were extremely balanced, I have come across a few who were authoritative and quite egotistical. A spiritual teacher with developed gifts must be careful to avoid such self-aggrandizing tendencies.

A common trait I've noticed amongst all the teachers I've met is that they tend to be quite charismatic, ego or no. Charisma is what hooks people into following a guru or a teacher. One's charm and magnetism is very strong to students and can unfortunately cloud the latter's vision. The teacher is put on a pedestal and sometimes worshiped. While it's good to admire and aspire to be like a teacher, remember that you are equally as magnificent and have the same potential. Influential teachers have excellent interpersonal communication skills, a positive quality we can all hope to acquire.

Telepathy

Everyone has the inherent gift of telepathy. Telepathy is the ability to have mind-to-mind communication without speaking. In other words, you can send a thought to another person and they will receive it. Many people develop this skill after being friends for a time because they're in sync with each other.

Telepathy is communication that occurs through pathways other than the normal senses of seeing, speaking, and hearing. It is in this form of communication that the use of sacred geometry comes in. Practice the following visualization as a start.

Become aware of the center of your forehead—your third eye center. Become aware of the center of your chest—your heart center. Draw a line from the center of your forehead to the center of your heart. Next draw a line from the center of your forehead and extend it out in front of you. Draw another line from the center of your heart out and extend it out in front of you until both lines meet at a point in front of you, creating the tip of a triangle. The line from your forehead to your heart is the base of the triangle, and the lines extending out in front of you form a point. This is what a telepathic link looks like geometrically. This is how a telepathic thought-form is transmitted, via the Divine Triangle.

The Divine Triangle is very simple to use. Imagine a triangle and place the base of it on you with one point at the heart chakra and the other point at the third eye. Still using your imagination, visualize the sides of the triangle that make the point directly out in front of you. Envision that your thoughts and emotions—your feelings—are travelling on the sides of the triangle and projecting toward the person, place, or thing you wish to telepathically communicate with. These thoughts and emotions can also be sent in the form of pictures.

My mother taught me how to develop my telepathic skills at a very young age. When I was a child, we did not have answering machines, pagers, or cell phones. My dad was a contractor and was often out of his office on job sites. In order to reach my dad during the day, Mom and I would imagine that Dad was picking up the phone and calling home. We would send the image of him going to a rotary phone and dialing SH5-1500. Then we would imagine the phone ringing and Mom walking over to pick it up. Sure enough, Dad would call soon after, usually within fifteen minutes to a half hour.

Practicing this technique developed my skills to such a degree that I often call someone exactly when they are about to pick up the phone to call me. In fact, I have really shocked and scared a number of my friends due to this uncanny ability. In some cases, I've called when people were discussing me, and they've wondered if I knew what they were saying. I must say, I haven't quite developed my telepathic skills to that degree—it would entail development of remote viewing skills, something I feel borders on inappropriate psychic "Peeping Tom" or eavesdropping! When I call someone who is thinking of me or having a discussion about me, an inspiration to pick up the phone and call them simply drops into my consciousness. I don't know why, and I am definitely not aware they are speaking of me.

The main stones associated with the third eye are indigo, purple, or clear stones like lapis lazuli, sodalite, clear quartz, selenite, apophyllite, and amethyst. When used with intention, all these stones have the inherent ability to help you further develop your intuitive skills.

The Six Clairs

The six clairs are my good friends and are very helpful in my life. I invite you to make them your friends as well. These clairs are the six senses you possess on an intuitive level. All people have these senses. To recognize them, you must acknowledge their existence, and then realize you already possess the ability to intuit. To use them is simply to get to know and develop them, just as you would exercise and develop a muscle. The "muscle" you're exercising is your intuition.

Intuition is the ability to know or sense something without using a rational or logical process. What you may think is rational and what I may think is rational are two different things. I was brought up to use my intuition. My mother called it ESP (extrasensory perception) and since this was a normal part of my life, for me, ESP *is* rational.

The upper three chakras—the throat, third eye, and crown—are responsible for these intuitive skills. The six clairs are clairvoyance (clear seeing), clairaudience (clear hearing), claircognizance (clear knowing), clairgustation (clear tasting), clairolfaction (clear smelling), and clairsentience (clear sensing). These six senses are part of each of the upper three chakras. As you develop these skills, you may feel you are making stuff up and calling it your intuition. Actually, the use of your imagination and making stuff up starts the process. It primes the pump so your intuition can come through. As the information comes, it may appear cryptic. With each of these intuitive skills, you will need to interpret the meanings of the messages you receive. You will need to decode and interpret the signs and symbols provided.

CLAIRVOYANCE

Clairvoyance is the intuitive skill people are most familiar with and strive for. Each intuitive skill is equally as important, but one skill is usually more predominant than another in each person. However, everyone possesses all six clairs and can develop all of them. Clairvoyance is the ability to receive intuitive messages through the vibration or energy of spiritual sight. This vibration resides primarily at the third eye, which is aptly named. When you use your clairvoyant abilities, you receive messages through visions in your mind's eye. This includes messages that come through dreams and daydreams.

CLAIRAUDIENCE

Clairaudience is the ability to receive messages or guidance through the sense of hearing. "Listen to the still, small voice within." Do you hear voices? The voice within is your connection with your higher self or your guides and angels. With proper development of this gift, you can learn to discern which voices bring valid, positive, helpful messages—and which ones don't. It's really no different than wisely choosing your friends.

You may "hear" a message, but not out loud like you hear someone speaking to you. Clairaudient messages are much more internal and subtle than actual sounds perceived in the normal sense;

however, you *can* receive clairaudient messages using your normal physical sense of hearing as well.

Unintentional eavesdropping is one way in which I've received answers to questions or prayers. For example, I have received information while standing in line at the grocery store. Consider the chances of being somewhere hearing two other people in conversation, saying things that answer your inner questions or calm your angst. A form of receiving angelic clairaudient message is through hearing a song on the radio or in your head containing a message pertinent to your life.

Claircognizance

Claircognizance is your natural ability to just know. You know because you do. If someone were to ask you how you know something, your response may simply be, "Don't ask me how, I just *know!*" It's important to trust inner knowing and apply it to life's situations. How many times have you known something, didn't trust your hunch, and followed a different direction, only to regret it? Your first impression is usually the best information. One of the important keys to intuition development is trust: trust your messages, dreams, visions, and gut feelings—often you will find you were right from the start.

Clairgustation

Clairgustation is the ability to intuitively pick up a taste in your mouth that provides a clue or insight for either yourself or someone around you. Medical intuitives often use this tool to identify their clients' physical challenges. A sickening, sweet taste, for example, may alert the intuitive to a diabetic condition.

A medical intuitive is a person who is able to apply all six clairs to assist in medical diagnosis. A famous medical intuitive was Edgar Cayce, who was called the Sleeping Prophet because he would fall into a deep trance to diagnose a person's medical challenges. During trance, Cayce would also provide treatments to assist clients' healing. While lying on his couch in a self-induced, sleep-like, meditative state, Cayce provided cures from things as simple as warts to life-threatening diseases.

I know a medical intuitive who uses both clairgustation and clairolfaction to diagnose an out-of-balance condition in the body. This intuitive is able to smell a scent and simultaneously experience a particular taste that alerts her to a client's condition, from candida, cancer, and liver disease to other health conditions.

CLAIROLFACTION

Clairolfaction is the ability to sense a smell that no one else around you smells. This smell provides some sort of guidance or clue to a situation at hand. I've heard of cases where people smelled the scent of roses and knew that the Virgin Mary had visited them through the scent. A scent itself may mean different things for different people, but the point is to apply the message to what is happening in your life at the moment in which you receive the sign.

Others have reported smelling their deceased mother's perfume when no one around them was wearing that scent (and, in fact, when that particular perfume was no longer manufactured). The scent of cigarettes, pipes, and cigars are a distinctive way loved ones on the other side will send a message to say they are nearby.

My first experience with clairolfaction occurred around 1990 in a yoga class being held at my shop. My yoga instructor was very connected with Haidakhan Babaji, who taught publicly from 1970 to 1984. From a Hindu perspective, Babaji taught how to live a life based on truth, simplicity, and love.

During yoga class, I smelled an unusual incense I had never smelled before. My shop had been open since 1988, and although I carried incense, I had never smelled this particular one. Then, in a vision in my third eye, I saw Babaji standing in a meditative state. At the time, I had only seen a picture of him once, and was unfamiliar with his energy and story, yet I knew who he was.

Of course, I shared my experience with my yoga instructor, and she encouraged me to read about him and get to know him. I found out later that Babaji is a master who would physically bilocate (the ability of one's consciousness to be in two different locations at once) and appear before his students. The gift of the scent helped me to expand my understanding of clairolfaction, and the vision of Babaji helped expand my spiritual path significantly.

CLAIRSENTIENCE

Clairsentience is the ability to sense or feel, and therefore know. The word *clairsentience* literally means "clear sensing." When you step into someone's energy field or space and are able to pick up feelings, insights, and information, you are using the intuitive skill of clairsentience. Clairsentience is the same as being extremely empathic.

Perhaps you remember the character Deanna Troi from *Star Trek: The Next Generation*. Troi had extrasensory abilities and could pick up the thoughts and feelings of alien guests on board the ship. She was an empath and a telepath. As a telepath, she was also able to sense beings' thoughts or what they wanted to communicate.

Medical intuitives are often empaths; they are able to feel pain or sense medically out-of-balance conditions within a person. I have a close friend, Melissa, who senses disease in those around her. Because she and I are the best of friends, she is also able to know when I am not feeling well. Once, when I was out of town teaching in another state, she realized that every time she thought of me, she sneezed. When I returned, she asked me if I'd had a cold or sneezed frequently while I was away. She was right—I had an upper respiratory infection and was sneezing and coughing the whole time I was away.

Clairsentients can also pick up vibrations of natural disasters, including earthquakes, tsunamis, tornadoes, and other weather conditions around the planet. Melissa will often know when an impending earthquake or another catastrophic condition will strike by the type of headache she has. There have been many times over the years where she would tell me that a very bad earthquake, solar flare, or volcanic eruption was about to occur and sure enough, within days, the information was confirmed.

A clairsentient uses psychometry, the ability to pick up vibrations from a person or an object and read or interpret those vibrations. In the TV show *Charmed,* Phoebe Halliwell had such an ability. Phoebe could touch an object and immediately get a vision that would help her with the challenge at hand. This ability is a combination of clairvoyance and clairsentience.

Everyone has the ability of clairsentience. Some of us are more developed in one sense than in another. Experiment with this simple exercise in psychometry.

Exercise

PSYCHOMETRY

Meet with a group of friends and acquaintances and pick one of them whom you hardly know. Ask to hold a watch, ring, key, necklace, or something the individual has owned for quite a while or that he or she carries around or wears often. Hold the object in your left hand, close your eyes, breathe, focus, and go inside yourself. Verbalize the thoughts, words, feelings, sensations, visions, tastes, or smells that come to you, regardless of whether or not they make sense. Have the courage to express what you receive.

After you are done sharing the messages, signs, or symbols you've received, ask the acquaintance to give you feedback. You will be amazed at your accuracy and how many of the items you touched upon have relevance in the person's life.

Billets

Another form used for giving "readings" is billets. *Billet* is a French word meaning "brief letter," and this section would not be complete without mentioning my colleague, Hoyt Robinette. Hoyt was trained and ordained by the Universal Spiritualists Association, and his ministry has taken him to most states in the country and to several international cities, where people have witnessed his great gift as well as his ability to channel spirits who speak in foreign languages through him. Billets are one of the tools he uses to assist in counseling and bringing comfort to the many people who have lost loved ones.

In a blindfold billet session, Hoyt will ask group participants to write the full names of several deceased friends or loved ones at the top of a 4 × 5-inch piece of paper. Participants are then instructed to write a question or two in the center of the paper, sign their full names, and fold the paper in half. Hoyt will tape his eyes shut with several pieces of tape and blindfold himself on top of that. He uses the billet as a focus so that he and Dr. Kenner, his powerful spirit guide, can contact a loved one's spirit. These beings from the spirit realm bring immeasurable peace, love, and guidance concerning situations mentioned on the billet. Hoyt uses a combination of psychometry and mediumship to receive answers.

Believe it or not, anyone can do this. I use billets as a tool for teaching students how to increase their confidence. This exercise proves to them that they have the ability to pick up vibrations from a person or object. If you really think about it, you do this all the time—have you ever met someone and instantly felt either attraction or repulsion? That reaction is your energy field or aura reading the other person's energy field. All your subtle bodies—mental, emotional, and spiritual—are sensing the other person on every level. Learning to trust your first impressions will save you a lot of time and trouble.

The Energy Field: Subtle Bodies

Each chakra's bands of energy envelop the physical body with subtle bodies known as the mental, emotional, and spiritual bodies. These energies have vibration and sound you can sense, feel, know, and read. In fact, your auric field is the reflection of light that emanates from these subtle bodies. All of your consciousness is contained within these subtle bodies, and it is these subtle bodies a psychic or intuitive draws upon when giving you a reading. Know that regardless of what a psychic says, the reading is based on your energy field in the present moment. You have free will to accept or change the prediction.

Body Parts Related to the Third Eye Chakra

The physical parts of the body directly related to the third eye chakra are the ears, nose, and eyes. The pineal gland, pituitary gland, and the brain are also associated with this center, a sensible association because these glands and organs assist in our capacity to know, hear, smell, see, sense, and taste. As previously mentioned, the upper three chakras energetically overlap.

BALANCING THE THIRD EYE CHAKRA

The use of positive thoughts combined with purple and dark blue gemstones will aid you in staying grounded and aligning your third eye. Amethyst will help with intuition, while lapis lazuli will help you stay grounded. Kyanite combined with selenite aligns you with the Divine to connect with the charismatic aspect of yourself while bringing higher-level sage wisdom through your consciousness. Apophyllite and quartz bring clarity and clear sight. The states of consciousness below are often associated with the third eye (and actually all three of the upper chakras).

Channeling

Develop your meditation practice in order to quiet your mind to strengthen intuition and prepare for channeling. Have the trust that your spirit guides and angels are available to bring you messages and guidance. Use clear quartz channeling crystals, a clear quartz Dow crystal, a cathedral library quartz, or any clear quartz crystal you designate as your channeling crystal. These clear quartz crystals are described in detail in chapter 9. Selenite and kyanite are also beneficial for connecting with higher states of awareness.

Egomania

Egomaniac vibrations can be balanced through self-observation and intended humbleness. The arrogance surrounding egomania requires that the individual either has an "Aha!" experience or is knocked down by a good ol' cosmic two-by-four. A clear quartz window crystal may be beneficial for observing and reflecting on how improvements in the personality can be balanced. (Chapter 9 on clear quartz offers further information on window crystals.)

Grounding

A constant connection with reality is crucial in order to stay focused and grounded in the real world. Development of the third eye and all six clairs can lead to airy-fairy, spaced-out behavior and attitudes. Ground messages in real time and real life, and apply them to daily living. Use lapis lazuli, sodalite, fluorite, and amethyst, as well as some black stones like black tourmaline, obsidian, and jet to stay focused.

Intuition

Develop your intuition through your intention. Become aware of all that is happening around you. Use your peripheral vision physically and intuitively. Incorporate purple stones such as amethyst, sugilite, and charoite to activate your intuitive senses. Deep blue stones such as lapis lazuli, sodalite, azurite, and kyanite assist in this inner development.

Telepathy

Telepathic linking, as described earlier in this chapter, involves the awareness of the energy of sacred geometry and the Divine Triangle. Use the geometrics of invisible lines of communication to send waves of thought to another being and be open to receiving messages as well. Use tabular quartz with "faden" lines to amplify this skill. (Further information about faden tabular crystals can be found in chapter 9.)

Gemstones for the Third Eye Chakra

The dark indigo, blue, and purple-colored stones assist in invoking intuition—all six clairs. Through the heightened awareness that can be attained through third eye development, personal growth and self-development can help you through your daily life. Use positive affirmations to enable better understanding of yourself, your friends, family, and coworkers, thereby improving your life.

The following affirmations are suggestions for focus while using stones for balancing your third eye. Remember, the stones are tools that will help you amplify your intention and maintain focus.

Agate

Use agate to ground your spiritual practice. Clear out incessant chatter with this stone. Use the dyed dark purple variety to activate your ability to go into a state of "no mind." Intend to live your spirituality and practice it in every aspect of your life.

Purple Agate Affirmation: I am grounded in my spirituality. Spirituality is integrated into my daily life. I am intuitive and insightful.

Amethyst

Amethyst is great for transforming any situation. It has been called the sobriety stone for a very long time and is associated with the breaking of bad habits. It's the perfect stone to use for the process of becoming a nonsmoker and a healthier person. It breaks harmful patterns and helps you live your life positively.

As amethyst is a crown chakra stone as well as a third eye stone, it is helpful for balancing both energy centers. Amethyst helps with dreaming—including nocturnal dreams, lucid dreams, and daydreams—for purposes of manifestation. It also helps to ward off nightmares or unpleasant sleeping challenges.

Amethyst Affirmation: I see, sense, feel, and know life is magical. I dream pleasant dreams. I release all habits no longer for my highest good. I have a great connection with my spirit guides and angels. I am profoundly clairvoyant.

Apophyllite

This sparkling gemstone comes in various forms and colors. For the third eye, use clear apophyllite points to gain mental clarity and improve the quality of your meditation experience. It is my favorite stone for placement on the third eye during a crystal alignment. An apophyllite as a solo stone on the third eye magnifies the meditation experience for a deeper, clearer, more profound practice. Good meditation practices develop your intuitive skills naturally. This inner reflection offers the ability to know, hear, see, sense, smell, and taste the truth of any given situation.

Apophyllite Affirmation: I am connected with the Divine. My meditation practice is easy and natural. I have profound meditation experiences. I am very intuitive. I get things done and accomplish all that needs to be accomplished. I have mental clarity.

Clear Quartz

Clear quartz crystal carries the full spectrum of light. Use the clear quartz at the third eye to increase perspective and visions. Clear quartz is a tool for amplification, so it will draw forth whatever intention you place inside the crystal.

Clear Quartz Affirmation: I see life from a greater perspective. My intuitive skills are increasing daily. I am extremely intuitive. I follow my internal guidance system.

Goldstone

There is a starry quality to goldstone that brings inner reflection as well as a reminder that you are a shining star. Gazing into goldstone reminds you to be all that you can be and allows your many talents to shine brightly. The blue goldstone stimulates your third eye center with its midnight blue color to open your intuitive senses, the six clairs.

Blue Goldstone Affirmation: I am extremely clairvoyant. I hear messages from my guides and angels all the time. I am grateful for and trust my inner guidance.

Lapis Lazuli

The deep, rich blue of lapis lazuli transcends time as it travels through ancient cultures of the past to the present day, providing peace, protection, grounding, and insight into the bigger picture of life. This stone was used by many ancient civilizations, but the Egyptians especially valued its qualities and incorporated it into jewelry, amulets of protection, and even a powdered pigment used for painting the ceilings of the burial chambers of the pharaohs. The lapis in your jewelry and the tumbled stones you carry in your pocket are still mined from the same geographical area of those ancient civilizations. From then until now, it is still the stone of intuition and truth.

Lapis lazuli contains white calcite, blue sodalite, and golden flecks of pyrite, as well as lazurite. Interestingly, lapis's pigment has been historically used in oil paintings as that vibrantly blue hue seen in many religious works. Calcite helps with change and transformation; sodalite calms and establishes a connection with higher knowledge; and pyrite grounds, protects, and strengthens prosperity and courage.

Use lapis lazuli for reducing inflammation, such as migraines and headaches. It is also useful pre- and post-surgery, for burns, arthritis, and any inflammatory disease. It also helps calm anger and irritability. Use lapis to displace upsets that can lead to inflammation with intention to regain the positive aspects of life.

On a spiritual level, lapis is an excellent tool for meditation. Place it on the third eye or hold it in your hand during meditation to assist you in maintaining focus while connecting with spirit guides, angels, or ascended masters.

Lapis Lazuli Affirmation: The wisdom of ancient cultures is stored within my cells, bones, and muscles, and I have access to it whenever I request it. My third eye is open exactly the right amount for me at this time in my life. I am extremely intuitive and receive messages and guidance all the time. I am calm and relaxed.

Selenite

Selenite is part of the gypsum family of gemstones. This soft rock is near transparent, with a shimmering translucent quality. The name of this stone is derived from the Greek moon goddess, Selene, due to its pearly, lustrous appearance. Selenite is a stone that, when used with conscious intention, aligns your physical structure—spine, bones, and muscles—as well as your spiritual body, to connect with higher wisdom and knowledge. Use selenite to improve your intuitive skills, develop connection with the Divine, and align with guides and angels. Kyanite and selenite work well together.

Selenite Affirmation: I am connected with the Divine. My intuitive skills improve every day. I am extremely intuitive. I follow the guidance I receive from my guides and angels. My physical structure is strong and aligned.

Sodalite

Sodalite is a rich, royal blue stone, a component of lapis lazuli. As such, a good deal of the information I've written about lapis applies to sodalite as well. In fact, it's sometimes challenging to distinguish between the two stones. Just look for the golden pyrite flecks—if there aren't any, the stone is most likely sodalite.

Sodalite is an anti-inflammatory stone. It reduces the frequency of migraines and headaches. It calms inflamed states of consciousness like anger, frustration, and agitation, as well as inflamed states within the physical body.

Sodalite Affirmation: I have calm emotions. My mind is clear and relaxed. I am intuitive. Any inflammation in my body, mind, or spirit is calm and in balance for my highest good.

Tiger's Eye

This stone usually occurs in reds and golden browns, and is typically used at the solar plexus, navel, and root centers. When it occurs in blue, it is also known as hawk's eye. A hawk's vision is far and wide. The hawk has great perspective, as it can view life from a higher perspective. The hawk is also considered one of the messengers of the Great Spirit in Native American spirituality. Therefore, the use of this stone can help you tune in to messages from your angels, spirit guides, and deceased loved ones and keep your eye on life's bigger picture. This stone is an excellent tool for developing spiritual sight, and although it may give the effect of a higher altitude, it is also grounding and protective.

Blue Tiger's Eye Affirmation: I am able to visualize my reality into being. I am very insightful and have extraordinary moments of inspiration. I receive and interpret the messages from the heavenly realm all the time. I can see the bigger picture of life and act accordingly. I am grounded and protected in my spiritual development.

Essential Oils for the Third Eye Chakra

This chakra of intuition and inner guidance explores the aspect of yourself connected with seeing the unseen, knowing what you didn't realize you knew, and sensing on multiple levels of consciousness. The focus on your third eye (the place behind the center of your forehead) develops your innate intuitive nature. The oils I've chosen for this chakra support your meditation practice and your ability to relax enough to trust your intuition.

Frankincense

Classically, frankincense, sandalwood, and helichrysum are spiritual oils that aid in meditation, focus, and higher states of consciousness. Frankincense oil increases your ability to breathe well. Use it for respiratory assistance. Much of the meditation work you do depends on controlling breath. Breathe deep. Breathe fully. Watch your consciousness become more alert and in the present moment.

Frankincense is used to invite and invoke positive energy to replace negativity, as well as to provide clarity. I use the resin form of frankincense in my mojo blend of sage, cedar, lavender buds, and osha root, along with many other plants and resins. I use this blend of herbs, called Margaret's Sacred Smudge blend, not only to clear sacred space, but to create sacred space as well.

When I burn resins, I watch the smoke rise and ask all four archangels to create and maintain the energy of love, light and well-being, and anything that is not aligned with that loving energy is forbidden from my sacred space. Likewise, although essential oils do not produce smoke, you can connect with your breath and smell the wonderful scents you have chosen as you invite and invoke the archangels Michael (east), Raphael (south), Gabriel (west), and Uriel (north). The archangels generate positive vibrations and protect your space.

Grapefruit

Grapefruit oil is cold-pressed from the peel. Grapefruit is renowned for reducing cellulite and is also helpful for mental exhaustion. Once again, as a citrus oil, it's naturally effective as an anti-infectious agent. Grapefruit is phototoxic, so take care if you plan on being in the sun. Citrus oils help bring about mental clarity. Mental clarity opens the door to good meditation experiences.

Helichrysum

Helichrysum is used for alignment with higher spiritual connections while relaxing the mind so it can focus on the present moment. Read a bit more under the crown chakra in chapter 8 for use in anointing the crown and third eye.

Lavender

Lavender can be used for every chakra—it has so many benefits. If I could choose only one essential oil to use, it would be lavender. Use lavender oil for headaches. Keep it handy in your purse or travel kit, as it is antibacterial, antifungal, antibiotic, and soothes burns. Use lavender for calming. Lavender is a stress reducer and is relaxing when you are at your wits' end. The purple energy of lavender can align you with pleasant dreams, including dreams that connect you with your angels, or dreams of insight and understanding. Use lavender for releasing persistent thoughts.

Peppermint

Peppermint can ease stomach upsets, so use it as a navel chakra oil as well as a third eye oil. It's a great scent to clear the sinuses and sweeten one's breath. I've used it to stop the itch from mosquito bites. Peppermint wakes up the mind, helps to bring mental alertness and clarity, and provides clarity and control for when that incessant inner chatter just won't quit! It's a good one to keep in the car for long road trips. This oil helps if you have a tendency to fall asleep when you meditate.

Rosemary

Rosemary oil has the ability to clear the sinuses and help you breathe easier. This oil assists students and people who do a lot of detailed mental work, and helps with memory functions. Smell it during class and while you are studying. Then smell it again when you are trying to remember the answers during the test. It's an aromatic cheat sheet, so use the oil, not an actual cheat sheet! Rosemary lifts your outlook on life and helps you connect with all that is good and positive. Its scent is clean and bright, and, because of its cheerful vibration, rosemary lifts the stupor of depression, so add it to your solar plexus oils as well.

Sandalwood

Sandalwood is derived from a fragrant wood by the same name. The scent helps you focus during meditation and prayer. Sandalwood instills peace and encourages spirituality. The scent of sandalwood is also an aphrodisiac.

———

Develop your intuitive abilities to become a powerful force of good in your family, in your community, and in the world. Self-awareness brings a more balanced view of yourself and your personality. Through self-understanding, you are better able to act frankly and confidently with others because of your sharpened intuitive skills. In order to achieve great things, focus and concentration are imperative. Combine those qualities with being in tune with the subtle (and sometimes not-so-subtle) influences surrounding you, and you'll have an improved ability to interact with others. It enables you to create a better world—one of love, truth, understanding, and compassion.

eight

GOLDEN WHITE LIGHT WITH VIOLET ENERGY AND THE CROWN CHAKRA

The crown chakra is at the very top of your head. This is the place where you would literally place a bejeweled crown if you were a king, queen, prince, or princess. Like all of the chakras, the energy of this chakra is expansive, and it encompasses the space around your whole head, overlapping energetically over the crown and throat areas. It's above you, behind you, and all the way around, matching up with the auric field of the rest of the chakras below, completing the energy field.

Envision a golden globe around the crown of your head. To help you do this, imagine halos you see portrayed in iconic artwork of saints and angels. Stop right now—pause and imagine you have this golden white light around the crown of your own head. Throw in a splash of pale violet. Imagine that the light around your head has sparkling light particles, and those particles are like antennas picking up the frequency of divine consciousness. Align with the belief that these particles help you tap into being a miracle worker aligned with divine consciousness.

The golden halo is a luminescent globe of sparkling particles of light surrounding your head. This halo is a reflection of your connection with higher wisdom and knowledge. Golden white energy with a tinge of violet, or the crown chakra, is located at the top of your head. The primary colors associated with this chakra are white, pale gold, and violet.

The Crown Chakra

Primary Colors: Pale golden light with violet, white
Stones: Amethyst, elestial quartz crystals, kyanite, lepidolite, moonstone, record keeper quartz crystal, selenite
Location: Around the crown of the head
Musical Note: B
Essential Oils: Benzoin, frankincense, helichrysum, sandalwood
Keywords: Access to higher consciousness and subconsciousness, higher intuition, miracle worker, magician, open to the Divine
Physical Body: Brain, nervous system, pituitary and pineal glands

Characteristics of the Crown Chakra

The improvement of our intuitive energy centers increases the potentiality of self-realization and movement to an enlightened status. The fulfillment of personal potential gives birth to unlimited possibilities. This unlimited potential expands into the realms of the mystical and esoteric. These spiritual gifts are latent within everyone, and it is up to each of us to awaken the talents. These gifts are vibrationally located within the crown chakra. Make a clear intention as to why you want to improve yourself. State how it will serve you and especially how it will serve others. We each have the mystical qualities of a magician, miracle worker, ascended master, and more. Which will you choose?

The Miracle Worker

The crown chakra is where you can shift your reality instantaneously. Siva Baba, a modern-day mystic and scholar originally from India, now living in the United States, says, "Every moment can open to a new reality." Using the vibration of a fully developed crown center, you are able to actualize this statement and know from this moment to the next, you have the ability to alter reality. Align with the vibration of being a miracle worker.

The crown chakra holds the vibration of the magician within you. You can re-create reality in a moment's notice. I'm not talking about the type of magician who can pull a rabbit out of a hat—I'm referring to the part of you aligned with the vibration Jesus worked with when he healed others.

The Magician

Merlin, that famous wizard of Arthurian legends, utilized the transformative purple vibration to perform miraculous feats. Merlin was a bard, wizard, prophet, and advisor to King Arthur. Due to his family heritage, Merlin was challenged with battling the opposing forces of good and evil that resided within him.

Many legends and myths surrounding Merlin exist. Here's my version: It begins with Ceridwen. Ceridwen was a supernatural character in the Welsh tradition. According to the *Mabinogion*, a collection of ancient Welsh stories of magic and mythology (including legends of King Arthur), Ceridwen gave birth to a son who was hideously ugly. So she created a potion in her cauldron to make him at least wise. According to legend, this potion had to cook for a year and a day; a young boy named Gwion stood by the cauldron, stirring it continuously. The first three drops of the resulting potion would impart great wisdom, and the rest was fatal. As fate would have it, while Gwion was stirring this mixture, three drops of the hot liquid dropped on his hand, and his natural instinct was to bring the burn to his lips to soothe it. In doing so, he accidentally ingested the potion.

Of course, Ceridwen was outraged, as the potion was meant for her son, and she began to chase Gwion, who turned himself into many animals to try to escape her relentless anger. When he turned himself into one type of animal, she would counter by turning herself into an opposing one. When he turned himself into a hare, she turned herself into a greyhound. When he turned himself into a fish and jumped into a river, she turned herself into an otter. Eventually, Gwion turned himself into a kernel of corn and Ceridwen became a hen and ate him.

When Ceridwen ate the kernel of corn, she became pregnant, fully knowing the child in her womb was Gwion, and she vowed to kill him upon birth. But once the child was born, she couldn't do it—he was so beautiful. Instead she sewed him up in a leather bag and threw him into the ocean. Gwion was found on a British shore by a Celtic prince (Elffin ap Gwyddno), and he grew up to be the legendary Taliesin. Merlin was Taliesin's son.

A central character in the Arthurian legends, Merlin was instrumental in transforming situations, as well as his own physical structure and the structure of others, to manipulate lives. Some of these manipulations were perceived by many as evil, but who is to judge? In view of the round table—a symbol of equality, unity, and oneness—perhaps the ultimate outcome was for the highest good. The main point here, without delving into the tales of King Arthur, is Merlin's abilities to shapeshift himself and others to orchestrate life in accordance to his personal connection with wisdom.

The Ascended Master

Another magical being, better known as an ascended master, is the Count of St. Germain, the carrier of the Violet Flame, the vibrational energy of alchemy. Both of these amazing men—Merlin and the Count of St. Germain—had very well-developed crown chakras, as they were able to create miraculous manifestations. The Count of St. Germain was an inventor, alchemist, composer, musician, adventurer, and much more. Some say he is immortal, although my research tells me he lived from 1710–84. And yet, my research also showed that he was present or available to people like Annie Besant (1847–1933), C. W. Leadbeater (1854–1934), and Edgar Cayce (1877–1945).

On a vibrational level, his immortal energy is present to this day. According to the St. Germain Foundation in Mount Shasta, California, he appeared in 1930 on the mountain's side to Guy Ballard, who channeled the "I AM" discourses. St. Germain is now considered to be an ascended master by many.

Some believe St. Germain is a modern incarnation of Merlin. There is a long string of theories on the various incarnations of these two—or should I say this one? My personal journey—through meditations, visions, memories, and past-life regressions—helped me to realize that Merlin, St. Germain, Francis Bacon, and Shakespeare were all the same being in various incarnations. Research has also shown he was a high priest in Atlantis, Plato, St. Joseph (the husband of Mary and guardian of Jesus), Proclus, Roger Bacon, an organizer behind the scenes of the Secret Societies in Germany, and Christopher Columbus. Whew! This guy was amazing—or should I say this guy *is* amazing?

Above is an example of a well-developed crown chakra, lifetime after lifetime. You, too, bring forward your knowledge and wisdom from previous incarnations. To bring this wisdom into awareness takes conscious direction to achieve the recollection of memories and knowledge. This achievement is something worth working toward. The development of meditation skills is an important factor in realizing the full scope of the awareness your personal consciousness has to offer.

Self-Realization

Unrealized power is a sign of a person with an out-of-balance crown chakra. A leader with enormous power and the potential to bring goodness to the planet but doesn't step up to the plate and deliver is a perfect example. Sometimes an out-of-balance crown chakra manifests as frequent migraines or headaches. This condition is the result of blocked energy.

An individual with the potential to be a powerful miracle worker will become frustrated if his or her power isn't put to use. Frustration is a typical symptom of the crown consciousness being repressed or blocked. Often, service to humanity will clear the frustration and thus the headaches.

I know an amazing artist who is able to sculpt, paint, draw, and create murals, portraits, computer-created graphic designs, and much more. For many years, she suffered from debilitating migraines. She did what she could to realign her physical body to eliminate the headaches, such as getting adequate rest and eating the right foods. As she stepped into her power and realized the magnitude and value of all she had to offer, her headaches diminished significantly. She truly is an extraordinary artist and visionary and I wouldn't be surprised if she brought some of her talents through with her from a previous incarnation.

Talents and challenges come with you from the many lives that precede your present incarnation. The challenges are a gift, as they are an opportunity to clear karma. You can't automatically remember all your lifetimes. If you could, you would go nuts! To remember all your lives at one time would be extremely confusing and too much to handle. Besides, there really isn't a benefit to remembering all your lives; you only need to remember what is relevant to this moment in your life as a tool for balance and wisdom.

The Akashic Records and Extraordinary Levels of Consciousness

The akashic records are an etheric place containing the records of all that has ever been, all that is now, and all potential and parallel realities, including the future. For example, in a parallel reality, you may have already read this book, written this book, or have complete knowledge and mastery of the contents of this book. The akasha (Sanskrit for "sky") is accessed through the crown chakra.

The integrative understanding and application of parallel realities provides you with opportunities for "do-overs" in order to repeat circumstances until you get it right. Potential experiences for your evolution thorough time and space are stored within the akashic records. Having access to your akashic records expands your awareness. From this expanded perspective, you can see and know the bigger picture and, when desired, draw upon a reservoir of potential or parallel realities. Access to the akashic records serves as a portal to step out of the confines of ordinary reality, much like the *nagual*, to understand the essence, or root causes and conditions, of the issue at hand. The definition of the word *nagual* is a person of knowledge who has the ability to navigate through realms and states of consciousness that are unknowable and imperceptible to most people. A nagual uses potential and parallel realities to obtain greater perspective. Once this perspective is attained, the nagual returns to ordinary reality with a concrete and integrated understanding of a situation, and is able to implement the realization into daily life.

This implementation of extraordinary realizations into daily life offers the opportunity to rise above normal human consciousness to a state of sagelike all-knowingness. This information can be extracted by the use of record keeper, channeling, elestial, cathedral library, or singing crystals. Singing crystals emit sounds and tones that can be heard on a clairaudient level that unlock encoded information. These crystals will be described in detail in chapter 9.

Past, parallel, and future information is stored within your cells, bones, muscles, and DNA, and is retrievable in any moment. As you work with various quartz crystals, they will either activate the knowledge and wisdom within you or download the missing information from your own akashic records.

Exercise

GOING UP? CONNECTION WITH HIGHER REALMS

Connect with the akashic records through intention and meditative focus. Use your ability to visualize and imagine combined with meditation. Be sure to have your journal and pen nearby. Relax your body. Calm your mind. Release thoughts except for your question or intention for connecting with the akashic records.

Imagine you are taking a journey up a special, sacred tower. The tower has an elevator that will take you to the 12th floor. Enter the elevator and imagine you are slowly ascending past each floor. Imagine your guardian angel or special guide is riding the elevator with you. Going up—level 1, 2, 3, 4, 5, 6, 7, 8, 9, 10, 11, and 12. The elevator doors open up to a glowing reception area where a council of elders is sitting at a long table. One of them acknowledges you and gives you special permission to enter the space beyond. As you focus your eyes and use your imagination, you realize there are rows and rows of records. It's your imagination, so these records can be in rows of books or rows of computers with huge databases. Approach the area where all the records are located, recall your intention, and allow the answers and insights to be "downloaded" into your consciousness. Now, trust that this download has occurred, and pick up your journal and pen. Start writing. Expect and know that the information you are writing in a free-flowing stream of consciousness is going to help you in your life. Keep writing until you feel the download is complete. Reread what you've written. If at first it appears the information seems less than what you had hoped for, have faith that each time you step into this process, you will receive clearer and better information.

Staying in Touch with Reality

To know all your lifetimes simultaneously would be like hearing voices from all your spirits, guides, or angels simultaneously—it would make you crazy. Yes, I mean that literally! Development of the crown and third eye center needs to be done with care, over time, and with great balance. A person can become catatonic if faced with an overload of information. Here is a story of an out-of-balance crown chakra.

In the year 2000, I went on a sacred journey with a number of fellow spiritual travelers to follow the Michael/Mary ley lines. The journey started in Marseilles, France, and continued across the English Channel into England. The trip culminated at Stonehenge, that famous group of standing stones on the Salisbury Plain in southern England.

Ley lines can be compared to the meridians (energetic pathways) in your body. Ley lines are the meridians in the body of Mother Earth. These lines of power correspond with many sacred sites on the planet, many of which have been found using various dowsing techniques. The Michael ley lines relate to the vibration of Archangel Michael, angel of Light, often portrayed slaying a dragon. The Michael ley line holds the masculine energy. The Mary lines relate to Mother Mary, Mary Magdalene, the Feminine Christ, and the lineage carrying Christ consciousness. The Mary ley line holds the feminine energy. The two ley lines flow and interconnect like a labyrinth throughout the landscape of the earth and are considered the sacred marriage of the masculine and feminine energy of the planet.

Connecting with these lines by literally walking and standing on them can shake you to your soul. For the purpose of sharing how an out-of-balance crown chakra manifests itself, I will tell you about one of the travelers on the journey who demonstrated strange behavior, "Julia." Julia was not very socially interactive. Many of us on this trip thought Julia was a bit timid, but we didn't think much of it at the time. As the trip progressed, we noticed she withdrew more and more from interacting with the rest of the group. We went in and out of churches, walked through remote landscapes, and visited various castles or ruins on a daily basis.

On our last day in France, before heading onto the ship that would take us across the English Channel, we stopped at a church that had extraordinarily high energy. According to one of the tour facilitators, this place holds the vibration where the Michael ley line ends in France. When we entered the church, we had some time to explore on our own. I was mesmerized by a statue of Mother Mary and realized I heard her speak to me as I stood before her. It was the closest experience of an apparition I had ever experienced. Other tour participants were toning, that is, using their voices, to send sacred sound throughout the church, while a musician played a flute in homage to this sacred place.

The tour director gathered us from various points around this church to the place where the ley line stops. As we approached the marker in the church floor where the ley line ended, we found Julia planted to it, facing a wall. She had automatically dowsed her way to the spot and had been standing there since we entered the church. The facilitator prompted her to move so others could experience the energy. From that moment on, Julia was not even close to being interactive with any of us. Unbeknownst to us, she had moved into a catatonic state and was not going to return—well, at least not during that leg of the trip. Julia no longer looked at anybody and would not respond to anyone. She kept her jacket on all the time with her hood up over her head. She appeared physically stiff.

The trip continued and we progressed to Tintagel in Cornwall, England, when Julia disappeared. She was gone overnight and finally found by the police in the wee hours of the morning walking aimlessly nearly four miles away from our hotel. It was then revealed that Julia had been in a mental rehabilitation facility immediately prior to the trip. She stopped taking her medications and the chemicals in her brain and body became out of balance.

The lesson of this story is that while Julia had demonstrated intuitive capabilities that allowed her to tune in to other realms, she was paradoxically tuned out of our reality. She consistently found the places where the ley lines were by using her body for dowsing. In retrospect, we realized that her timid nature was misinterpreted. She was actually retreated into her own world while receiving messages connected to another level. The challenge for anyone having extrasensory ability is to stay grounded and balanced in the society in which we live.

It is important to maintain a healthy barrier that keeps you in this reality while you develop your third eye and crown. This occurs naturally when you develop the intuitive centers over time. The development of the intuitive centers can go to your head (pun intended) and create an overinflated ego. Maintain a humble nature as your gifts increase. The key to preserving your humility is to remember that these spiritual gifts are flowing *through* you, not coming *from* you. The divine will, not your will, is working to create miracles for yourself and others.

Use kyanite with selenite as a good mix for connecting with divine energy and allowing the love to flow through you. Maintain the intention that higher consciousness flows into you through the crown of your head and flows out through your eyes, words, thoughts, and reactions, as well as your palms, for hands-on healing.

What Is Your Intention?

When you work with the three upper chakras, focus on serving others. Serving others encompasses genuine care and concern without expectation of any return. As you connect with the spiritually focused chakras, your level of integrity and authenticity becomes paramount. Spiritual focus requires you to be the best you can. This includes impeccability.

To be impeccable can be defined as being incapable of wrongdoing. In order to achieve this state consistently, you must observe your stated intentions as well as your underlying intentions. These are referred to as your first and second intentions respectively. For example, when you seek out a friendship with someone, there is often more than one layer of why you want to be friends with that person. Often these layers are hidden below the surface and are unconsciously held within.

Through inner searching, honesty with yourself, and true integrity, you are able to uncover the different levels of intention. The crown is the place of mastery, the miracle worker, divine consciousness, and higher intuition. In order to truly step into this level of mastery, the underlying intentions should be observed, dealt with, and cleared.

Let's use the example of befriending new people. What is the underlying intention behind your connection? On the surface you might argue the point that you really like them and would have chosen them for friends regardless of their connections or affiliations. As you delve into your consciousness with honesty, you may uncover you really want to be friends because of a person's network of associates. If that network could bring you more business connections, then the second intention of the friendship is to make more money, even though the first intention may have initially been a legitimate friendship connection.

There is nothing wrong with having a second intention. It is advisable, though, to observe yourself to uncover the second intention. Be clear and honest with yourself about the reasons you are making connections, and maintain honesty in the relationship as to the mutually beneficial second intention. Do not draw people to you solely seeking friendship when clearly you have other layers of intention as well. This consciousness of layers of intention resides in all three of the upper chakras—throat, third eye, and crown.

Body Parts Related to the Crown Chakra

The physical parts of the body directly related to the crown chakra are the pituitary and pineal glands, the brain, and the nervous system. These parts of your makeup are essential for being grounded and balanced. As previously mentioned, the upper three chakras overlap energetically and systemically.

BALANCING THE CROWN CHAKRA

The crown chakra becomes enlivened when you focus on receiving divine vibrations from higher-level consciousness. Maintain an intention to open the channel at the crown of the head to actualize your innate abilities using clear quartz, amethyst, selenite, and elestial quartz. Realize that the intention is to let the Divine flow *through* you to be an instrument of good in the world.

Ascended Master Connection

Diligence and discipline are required to maintain a consistent meditation practice that will aid you in accessing higher consciousness. Hold the intention to maintain a tuned and aligned chakra system for a fully developed yet balanced crown chakra. Use quartz crystals such as elestials or record keepers (see the next page under "Gemstones for the Crown Chakra" for description) to access higher states of awareness. Selenite and kyanite work well together for meditation and channeling. Herkimer diamonds, kunzite, apophyllite, amethyst, sugilite, lepidolite, and charoite assist in aligning and balancing the crown chakra.

Migraines

As discussed earlier, migraines often manifest when you aren't realizing your full potential and full power. To bring this into balance, use the following gemstones: lapis lazuli, sodalite, selenite, kyanite, and apophyllite. Citrine and other yellow stones can aid in raising self-esteem for the necessary courage to step into your power.

Mental Imbalances and Emotional Mood Swings

The brain and the mind are tricky to deal with if they fall out of balance. If no chemical imbalances are evident, the use of lepidolite with rubellite inclusions can realign the swinging pendulum. Lepidolite is made up of lithium mica. Don't place this stone into your drinking water—instead, carry it with you daily. Sleep and meditate with lepidolite. Look at it and hold it close. Allow the lithium's energy to realign you. Other stones that may assist are chrysocolla, moonstone, and peacock ore. Peacock ore is also known as chalcopyrite, bornite, and peacock copper. Use peacock ore to see the full spectrum of life and to be grounded in reality while allowing higher vibrations to flow through you.

GEMSTONES FOR THE CROWN CHAKRA

The energy of the golden globe around your head connects you with your higher self and higher awareness. We each have the potential to be a miracle worker and magician, and create happy, healthy lives. The stones that follow are to be used with positive affirmations. Focus on the suggested affirmations while using them for activating and amplifying your crown chakra. Amplify your intention and maintain focus.

Amethyst

The transformative nature of amethyst can align you with the magical power of intention. Amethyst is a crown chakra stone as well as a third eye stone. I've used the amethyst vibration and the Violet Flame of St. Germain for transforming all types of negative situations. I remember one situation, a trip I took to Italy and Germany, where amethyst and the purple light energy of the Violet Flame came in handy. I somehow ended up traveling with someone who was less than kind, to say the least. Her actions and words reminded me of bully, bratty girls in grade school. It was unfathomable to me that at my age, I somehow manifested this bizarre traveling companion.

I used the transformative power of amethyst by wearing an amethyst bead necklace and imagined I was enveloped in a cocoon of the transformative power of the Violet Flame of St. Germain. It took a few days, but the trip changed, because she decided to go to another part of Europe while I stayed in Germany with friends. I never had to see her again! The power of intending only good things, combined with wishing her well on her way out of my life, shifted the vibration by using loving intentions. Love heals all situations.

Use amethyst to help transform your life when you may feel like you are stuck or trapped in a job or relationship. Allow yourself to come to the realization that you love yourself more than any job or relationship. Use conscious intention to manifest the manner in which you want to be treated and loved, and it will become a reality.

Amethyst Affirmation: I now transform my life easily and with grace. I see, sense, feel, and know that life is magical. I activate the miracle worker within. I have a great connection with my spirit guides and angels. I am profoundly clairvoyant.

Elestial Quartz Crystal

The multiple terminations of the elestials offer you the opportunity to uncover deeper parts of yourself.

The legend of the elestial quartz crystal states that elestial quartz crystals were brought through the atmosphere by the angelic realm. The multiple triangles on the surface and within the interior structure of this crystal activate stored memory within your physical brain. The elestial crystal assists in deepening the connection with the divine source of all wisdom and knowledge.

I keep my collection of elestials nearby when I write. When I pause to contemplate or reflect on what is coming through, I often unconsciously pick up one of the elestials to gaze into as part of my writing process. Therefore, I can now say elestials assist writers and artists in the creative process.

Elestial Affirmation: My angels surround me and assist me all day, every day. I hear, sense, feel, and know the guidance from my angels and spirit guides. I have balanced emotions. I am connected with ancient wisdom. Ancient wisdom is stored within me and I access it. I am inspired.

Kyanite

Blue Kyanite is used to connect with higher realms of consciousness. Use this blue stone to develop and balance the third eye and the crown chakras. It offers a clear connection with divine wisdom, spirit guides, and angels through the chakras.

Kyanite is known for its ability to align the chakras without any conscious direction. Of course, carrying or using the stone with conscious intent provides a more profound effect on chakra realignment. Kyanite works well with selenite to bring through wisdom from the divine source to be used in daily life.

Kyanite Affirmation: All my chakras are balanced and aligned with each other. I live my life harmoniously. I am a channel of divine wisdom. I easily connect with all that is.

Lepidolite

Lepidolite is a pastel violet stone composed of lithium mica. Sometimes rubellite, also known as pink tourmaline, is included within it. The lithium in the lepidolite provides a vehicle to rebalance intense mood swings and out-of-balance emotions. Lithium is a chemical used in mood-stabilizing psychiatric drugs for bipolar disorders to suppress the swings between depression and mania. It is also often used in cases of borderline personality disorder.

Do not place this stone in drinking water, as the lithium will leach into the water and be physically harmful to you. Instead, use the vibrational essence of the stone combined with your intention to rebalance the stressful experience of mood swings and uncontrollable crying or hysteria. To use the vibrational essence, carry the stone with you and place it in your pillow case while you sleep. Generally, keep the lepidolite nearby to maintain your intention to restore balance and harmony to your life. (The essential oil of sweet marjoram can also help during these times of despair.)

The inclusion of rubellite teams well with lepidolite to replace the angst with love and well-being. Add another pink stone like rhodonite, rose quartz, kunzite, or rhodochrosite for amplification of love if your lepidolite doesn't contain rubellite. Lepidolite manages the energy of the third eye and crown chakras. The energetics of this gemstone offer a vibrational alternative that recalibrates the chemical imbalances when used in the early onset of challenging times.

Lepidolite Affirmation: I have balanced emotions. All is well. I am love and I deserve love. I consistently maintain a balanced and joyful outlook on life.

Moonstone

Moonstone comes in many colors, including white, peach, beige, brown, and black. When the light refracts in such a way as to reveal rainbows within the stone, it is called rainbow moonstone. The reflective sheen from moonstone offers an avenue for exploration and development of your feminine aspect. Everyone has both masculine and feminine energy. Feminine energy is receptive and passive, and involves the state of "being" as opposed to the state of "doing." It is beneficial to develop and acknowledge your feminine nature while striving to achieve balance between it and masculine energy. This is part of developing a relationship with yourself.

Connecting with your feminine energy can be challenging, especially if you are accustomed to constantly taking action. The feminine is about nonaction. It is doing nothing. It is being an empty vessel ready to receive. The state of feeling and expressing emotions is feminine by nature. Allowing the part of your consciousness that senses to surface improves your connection with the Divine Feminine. The feminine energy is "being," intuitive, patient, contemplative, nurturing, receptive, right brain, creative, calm, and allowing.

Moonstone is a beneficial stone for mothers and mothers-to-be. It is helpful for the reproductive functions, including fertility, childbirth, menstruation, and menopause. It's beneficial for connecting with the Divine Mother at the crown chakra and with the Earth Mother at the navel chakra.

Moonstone Affirmation: I allow love. I am an empty vessel ready to receive insight and wisdom. I flow with grace and am in alignment with my feminine energy.

Record Keeper Quartz Crystal

This quartz crystal has triangular or pyramid-shaped markings etched onto various faces of the crystal. "Record keepers" hold records within them. They also activate records and knowledge stored in your DNA, cells, bones, and muscles. To work with a record keeper crystal, spend time with it. Hold it in your hands whenever possible. Stare at the faces and allow the light to refract off of them to reveal the teachings hidden within you and the crystal. You will find you have information and knowledge flowing in and around you whenever you need it.

Record keeper crystals help you access the akashic records. The akashic records are etheric or energetic libraries that hold all that has have ever happened in the past, all that is presently occurring now, and all the potential realities of the future, including the many variations of possibility.

Record Keeper Affirmation: I have all the information and knowledge I need available to me. I know how to obtain the guidance or help for any project I undertake. I am connected with the wisdom of the akashic records.

Selenite

This soft gemstone is strong and powerful for connecting the crown chakra with higher intuition, higher consciousness, and the part of you that is a miracle worker. Its white coloring amplifies the white light in the halo part of your aura by increasing the luminosity that activates the light particles. Use kyanite and selenite in combination for alignment with the wisdom of the ages.

Selenite is a tool for reiki practitioners to aid in the alignment with the universal life force. Reiki is a Japanese technique used for stress reduction and relaxation that also promotes healing.

Selenite realigns the spinal column when used with conscious intention. Use selenite in your meditative practice and imagine white light filling your spinal cord. Selenite is good for the body's main structure, including muscles, tendons, ligaments, and bones. It helps you connect with the ancient knowledge stored in the structure of your bones.

One variety of selenite is red selenite, which actually looks orange. Red selenite helps ground vibrations as they move from the crown through the entire chakra system. It is beneficial at the root, navel, and solar plexus chakras for the integration of higher spiritual wisdom.

Selenite (White) Affirmation: I am aligned with the Divine. I am a spiritual being of divine love and divine light. I channel messages of hope and grace for myself and others. My spine, bones, tendons, and muscles are healthy, strong, and aligned. The wisdom of ancient cultures is stored within my cells, bones, and muscles, and I have access to it whenever I request it. *Red Selenite Affirmation:* I am grounded and focused in my spirituality. Spiritual wisdom is integrated into my daily life.

ESSENTIAL OILS FOR THE CROWN CHAKRA

The crown chakra is your connection with your higher self, divine consciousness, and the part of you that is a miracle worker. It is the link to higher intuition. It is the center of awareness used to channel ascended masters and teachers who have attained enlightenment. The oils used for awakening this chakra can assist you in further aligning with this higher wisdom.

Benzoin

Benzoin has a warm, deep, rich, nurturing scent. It is a thick, viscous substance that possesses a vanilla-type scent. It has been used for protection, purification, and prosperity for many centuries. Benzoin is used as a fixative for maintaining a scent or stabilizing the scent of other oils. Like frankincense and myrrh, it is a sap from a tree. All of the oils and resins derived from the "blood" of a tree have strong, important work to do. Dragon's blood, amber, and copal (discussed in chapter 1 in the section on smudging) are all derived from the sap or "blood" of a tree.

Benzoin can be helpful in an emotional crisis and is an antidepressant. Depression is a crown, third eye, or a solar plexus chakra issue. Consider making a synergistic blend with benzoin as one of the ingredients, based on the specific situation. Benzoin stimulates the conscious mind, and with that stimulation, it offers the user an opportunity for self-observation and the shifting of awareness.

Frankincense

For more than three thousand years, frankincense has been in use for spiritual purposes. Its aroma heightens spiritual awareness and is an excellent tool for meditation practice. Add a drop to a carrier oil, and then place a few drops on the top of your head. You can also place a drop in a diffuser to disburse the scent. As with all oils mentioned in this section, use an oil in combination with a crystal alignment to expand balancing potentials.

Helichrysum

Helichrysum is also known as immortelle. I use this oil for anointing babies during blessing ceremonies by mixing it with tap water and holy water associated with the Virgin Mary. It is also the oil used when a person is preparing to pass over to the other side, as the oil aids in transitioning from one realm to another. Helichrysum lessens the effects of shock, fear, and phobias, so it makes sense to use it to aid humans entering and exiting the planet.

Frankincense, helichrysum, and sandalwood are also used for the crown chakra. These oils are superb for aligning with the Christ part of you. They help you connect with all the masters who have walked this planet and have reached greater heights of enlightenment. These spiritual oils aid in focused meditation and higher states of consciousness.

Sandalwood

Sandalwood helps the mind release ties from the past. Its value also includes the ability to assist one in releasing obsessions. It relaxes the mind and releases tension. Interestingly, frankincense and sandalwood have many of the same qualities in that they both calm the mind, refresh and uplift the attitude, and free the mind of past obsessions and anxiousness. These oils aid in aligning you with being in the present moment, thereby liberating you to achieve higher states of spiritual awareness.

———

The portal of heightened spiritual awareness enters through the crown. That being said, upholding a balance of each chakra from the base of the spine to the top of the head is genuinely the key to that portal. No one chakra is more important than another. As we strive for enlightenment, it is important to stay focused, objective, and evenhanded in our distribution of attention for each chakra.

The rainbow body needs the establishment of the red vibration to secure the foundation. The orange energy must be in place at the navel to protect and stabilize the ability to birth and create on this planet. The yellow of the solar plexus wants to shine brightly to empower any process with enthusiasm and joy. The green and pink of the heart brings love as the core essential to all aspects of life. The pastel blue of the throat expresses the truth in all that is. The indigo at the third eye is the doorway to inner realms, and the vibrant golden globe creating the halo at the crown is like an antennae that broadcasts and receives what is omnipresent.

nine

THE QUARTZ FAMILY
AND THE
FULL SPECTRUM OF LIGHT

*C*lear quartz can be used as a tool to change energy from one form to another, or, in other words, amplify or transmute energy. It can also be used to store, transmit, or receive information based on your specific intention. Therefore, focus on love, light, and well-being as a mantra when working with clear quartz crystals to amplify and stabilize positive conditions.

Quartz crystals were used in the first radios. Quartz was the heart of telecommunication equipment in the 1940s. The discovery of piezoelectricity (the generation of electricity or of electric polarity in crystals when under stress) by the Curie brothers in 1880 opened a doorway to advances in telecommunication for use in government technology as well as small and large industry. Radio technology gives us the ability to select a channel and attune to or stabilize a particular frequency in order to receive a broadcast. Apply that basic principle to your connection with the spiritual realm and you will see why holding a quartz crystal can help you stay focused when you meditate or tune in to the cosmic forces.

Many spiritual counselors keep a clear quartz crystal nearby when they do a reading or healing to assist alignment with higher knowledge. Channeling points are ideal crystals to use when counseling others. Geometric configurations on the faces of a channeling point are conducive to attracting wisdom, a process which will be explained more fully later in this chapter.

Use a clear quartz crystal while studying to help you maintain focus and retain the information. I designated one of my clear quartz points as my study crystal while studying for an exam. I held it in my hand or placed it on my desk while I studied and took it with me to the exam. When I could not recall an answer, I would redirect my attention to the crystal in my pocket and instantly remember. I had already done the work by studying the information. Therefore, in reality, it was stored within me. The crystal served as a focusing tool and as a reminder that I could retrieve that information. The work must be done to achieve results in whatever you do.

Marcel Vogel and Vogel-Cut Crystals

When sharing information about quartz crystals, I always introduce Marcel Vogel into the conversation. Marcel Vogel (1917–91) was a phenomenal man and scientist who developed a variety of products, including fluorescent crayons and the psychedelic colors popular in posters. Marcel was a senior research scientist with IBM for twenty-seven years. He received more than a hundred patents for his inventions, including the magnetic coating for the hard disc drive. Marcel was an expert in luminescence, phosphor technology, magnetics, and liquid crystal display (LCD) technology. Most notable to me, however, Marcel was instrumental in bridging science and spirit with his research on quartz crystals.

In the short time I trained with Vogel, I learned more about crystals than I had in all my years beforehand. He reaffirmed what I had learned as a child about the power of the mind, its thoughts, and the power of love to heal and rebalance the body. As has been discussed throughout this book, everything is energy, including thoughts. Vogel discovered that thought can be pulsed, transmitted, and stored within a crystal (see the Reference section for more information about Vogel's experiments and life work). With these discoveries came the advent of using crystals and gemstones for healing and rebalancing body, mind, and spirit.

Marcel's contributions were innumerable. For me, the most significant was the manner in which he cut quartz crystals. He developed a very specific way of faceting quartz that exponentially increased the crystal's power. Vogel-cut crystals were developed to amplify and cohere thought for use in the structuring and purification of water, structuring of wine for rapid aging, and realignment of the body for purposes of healing.

CLEARING YOUR QUARTZ CRYSTALS

Marcel Vogel said it was possible to clear a crystal using breath and intention. It's the easiest and most effective way to clear a crystal. What's really great is that you don't need accessories nor do you need to buy a thing. Use your predominant hand to roll the crystal in a clockwise direction while pressing firmly on each facet. This creates a piezoelectric charge. Piezoelectricity is simply the ability of some materials, including crystals, to have electric potential when under stress.

Once this charge is established, place the forefinger of your predominant hand onto the tip of the crystal, if possible. Use your other hand to create a cross current by placing your forefinger and thumb on the opposite sides of the body of the crystal. Breathe in through your nose, form the intention to clear the crystal, and while holding your breath, allow the thought-form of your intention to clear the crystal to increase. Exhale forcefully through your nose. The force of the exhaled breath is similar to the force of a sneeze or strongly blowing out a candle. The intention for clearing a crystal can be something like, "My intention is to clear this crystal. Release whatever is not for my highest good and the highest good of all concerned." Repeat this process for each pair of facets of the crystal. Quartz is a six-sided gemstone, so you need to repeat this process three times, as you're holding two sides at a time.

To charge the crystal, simply hold it in your dominant hand; roll the crystal in a clockwise direction while pressing firmly on each face; and form the intent to charge the crystal with love, light, and well-being. Pulse that intent with your breath.

You actually don't have to have the crystal in your hand to clear it. In some instances, you may have a large assortment of crystals that you'd like to clear or a crystal that is too big to hold in your hand. To clear a number of crystals at the same time, look at each of the crystals you want to clear and make the strong intention that all these crystals will be cleared. Then follow the same process as indicated above, the only difference being that you don't hold the crystals in your hands. A strong and focused intention is crucial to effectively clear your crystals. Once you have formed the intention, remember to pause for a few seconds and hold your breath. Next, forcefully exhale and direct the breath toward the crystals you wish to clear.

I clear all the crystals in my shop using breath and intention. You don't even have to be at the location of the crystals that need to be cleared. Breath and intention and telepathy and visualization performed remotely are equally effective. There have been times that I have cleared, reset, and recharged the shop through the intention of love, light, and well-being from far away using telepathic linking and visualization. You can clear your house, office, or car in the same manner. The idea is to hold the intention and imagine, visualize, and *know* it is effective.

TELEPATHY

Telepathic linking is the process of hooking up your heart and mind to the heart and mind of another person, place, or thing. You can use telepathy for clearing and charging crystals or other objects as well. In the case of clearing and recharging my shop, I telepathically link and imagine all the crystals and merchandise being cleared, using the intention and breath process previously described. Then, using the same process, I also charge all of the crystals and all of the objects in the shop by imagining they are vibrating with love, light, and well-being. I can do this from anywhere in the world. I establish the intention that the shop is continuously self-clearing and all who enter it will feel a sense of well-being and love. I visualize that everyone who enters the shop has the realization of how wonderful it feels to be there. I imagine them audibly sighing in relief and comfort. I see, sense, feel, and imagine the customers commenting to themselves or someone else how wonderful the store feels. The further you go with your visualization and imagination, the better!

Other methods for clearing crystals can be used. You may enjoy the ritual of smudging your stones with the various herbs and resins. Use salt "baths" to clear your crystals, but don't leave them in salt for long. Just pass them through the saltwater, rinse, and put them aside to dry. You should remove them immediately afterwards, as polished stones often lose their shine after sitting in saltwater.

You can also run tap water over your crystals with the intention of clearing them. Other methods for clearing are to put them in the moonlight or sunlight. You can take them to the beach and rinse them in the ocean, but beware, because crystals often return to Mother Earth in this way! I've lost quite a few rocks I've taken to the ocean for a dip. Although the other methods mentioned above are effective, I recommend Vogel's method of using your breath and intention as the best way to clear your crystals. Regarding amplifying energy and thoughts, Vogel says, "The crystal is a neutral object whose inner structure exhibits a state of perfection and balance. When it's cut to the proper form, and when the human mind enters into relationship with its structural perfection, the crystal emits a vibration which extends and amplifies the power of the user's mind. Like a laser, it radiates energy in a coherent, highly concentrated form, and this energy may be transmitted into objects or people at will."

Whether or not a quartz crystal is cut, it is a tool that magnifies intention and thought. To test this theory, hold a pair of dowsing rods toward a person holding a crystal who has been instructed to think the words *love*, *light*, and *well-being*. I use two metal L-shaped rods with a plastic tube on the handles. To dowse, hold the rods by the plastic tubing so they can swing freely. The rods measure subtle energy. If the energy is clear and good, they will swing open. If the energy is negative or blocked, the rods will swing toward each other and cross.

To measure how thoughts affect your energy field while holding a quartz crystal, ask someone to participate in an experiment with you. To begin the exercise, face your partner and stand approximately ten feet apart. Have one person hold a quartz crystal charged with love while the other holds a dowsing rod in each hand. The dowsing rods will swing open of their own accord as the crystal holder's energy field expands with positive love. Repeat this experiment, but have the crystal holder think of something sad or negative. The dowsing rods will barely open, if at all, or will cross towards each other, demonstrating how a person's energy field closes down and contracts. Repeat both experiments without the crystal to measure the difference in the expansion and contraction of the energy field.

You can use a similar exercise, called kinesiology, to determine if a crystal, food, vitamin, or any other thing is good for you. As Dr. George Goodheart says on his website, "Applied kinesiology (AK) is a form of diagnosis using muscle testing as a primary feedback mechanism to examine how a person's body is functioning. When properly applied, the outcome of an AK diagnosis will determine the best form of therapy for the patient. Since AK draws together the core elements of many complementary therapies, it provides an interdisciplinary approach to health care." (www.appliedkinesiology. com).

Kinesiology is a simple technique that can be done in a variety of ways. Stand strong with your feet firmly planted. If you practice yoga, stand in the mountain pose and just breathe. Place one arm out to the side and have someone press down on your arm as you resist the pressure. This establishes a base measurement of the strength of your arm.

Next, hold the thought of something that makes you really happy and have the person press down on your arm again. Observe your strength. Now add a crystal you have charged with love, light, and well-being. Hold the crystal to your chest and ask the question "Is this crystal good for me?" Repeat the test. Observe your strength. If your arm stays strong, the crystal is good for you.

Now try this: take a cell phone and hold it to your chest and ask, "Is this cell phone good for me?" Watch what happens. Does your arm get weak or does it stay strong? Whenever I've done this test for myself or another, the arm significantly weakens.

When you don't have someone near to push your arm down, you can do this experiment. Your whole body will dowse the energy and be reflected in your physical reaction. Stand firm, hold an item to your chest, and ask if the item is good for you. If it's good for you, you'll sway slightly toward it; if it's not, you'll sway slightly away from it. I use this technique when standing in front of many brands of vitamins and I can't choose which brand is best for my body. People may wonder what I'm doing, but I just smile at them, and they smile and move away from the crazy lady hugging vitamin bottles!

Where Do Quartz Crystals Come From?

Quartz crystals grow in cluster formations in the veins of mountains. It takes millions of years for the growth of a crystal cluster, a period of time so long that it is almost incomprehensible to us.

The name "crystal" originates from the golden ages of ancient Greece. The Hellenes believed that the crystals—*krystallos*—were pieces of ice from the mountains that had turned to rock. They froze so strongly, they would never thaw and melt.

Individual crystals break off from larger clusters or matrixes into single points. Most clear quartz crystals are packed in clay found within mountain veins. Some crystals, such as Herkimer diamonds, form within concretions of hard rock. Clear quartz crystals form perfectly in the earth. Most crystal points you find at stores are naturally formed and uncut by human hands. The way you see them is exactly how they came out of the ground.

Quartz crystals often have a film of red stain from Mother Earth's clay packaging. To remove the clay stains on quartz crystals, place them within a pot of heated water with oxalic acid. Oxalic acid can be purchased from a chemical supply company or at a mine site. Miners themselves clean many crystals at once using large vats or pots over a fire outdoors. The crystal points and clusters are placed on metal shelving within the vat with the oxalic acid water mixture. It made quite an impact on me to see these huge black pots in the midst of rows and rows of wooden work tables outdoors under the trees in Mount Ida, Arkansas, at the Ocus Stanley and Son Crystal Mine.

Some points are polished or cut. Many crystals mined in Brazil are polished or specifically faceted. The Vogel-cut crystal is cut and polished as the name indicates, but many gemstone cutters follow a crystal's natural lines and polish the crystal on its facets. Such methods remove markings and etchings and reveal a crystal's inherent clarity.

Tumbled stones are another form of polished stone. Tumbled stones are small round stones that have been polished within a tumbler. A tumbler is a barrel with a variety of hard grit or sand. Rough stone is placed within the barrel and rotated until the rough edges are removed. During a final phase of tumbling, the stone is polished. Tumbled stones transform rough, dense stones into beautiful gemstones. They are easy to carry in your pocket, purse, or briefcase. They are effective for use in a crystal alignment for yourself or another.

THE MANY FACETS OF CLEAR QUARTZ CRYSTALS

Natural clear quartz crystals are six-sided crystals. The sides are the facets on the body of the crystal and the faces are called facets on the termination of the crystal. The crystal faces' formations reflect its inherent qualities. In this section, you'll learn about the varying faces and facets of quartz crystals. I encourage you to look at your own crystal collection, if you have one, to identify and experience the energy of the varying types of clear quartz points as you read.

CATHEDRAL LIBRARY QUARTZ

Cathedral library crystals align you directly with God. Just as you might enter a cathedral or temple to commune with the higher forces, this crystal activates the part of you aligned with inspiration and higher wisdom. As with record keepers and elestials, this quartz configuration assists you in tapping into the akashic records. Sit in meditation with a cathedral library crystal to receive information and wisdom from a master guide or a wise sage.

The appearance of a cathedral library crystal is distinctive. It's a six-sided single terminated quartz point with many faces on the point. There are some similarities to elestial quartz or self-healed crystals. The crystal appears to have many terminations (pointed tips) at one end. There are many triangular facets formed by the many points melded together, creating terminations that spiral upward like the spires of a cathedral.

Channeling Quartz Crystals and Dow Crystals: Seven-Three-Seven-Three-Seven-Three

Channeling quartz crystals have an opposing seven-sided face and a three-sided face. This configuration offers the vibration of balance. The numerological vibration of the seven aligns with the seven chakras and seven levels of human consciousness. The numerological vibration of the three aligns with body, mind, and spirit.

The earliest information published on crystals and gemstones was channeled by Jane Ann Dow; hence, the Dow channeling crystal is named after her. Dow collaborated with Katrina Raphaell when Raphaell was preparing to teach a crystal healing class. Raphaell published her books as a result of compiling the information that she and Dow received collaboratively. Both are forerunners in bringing information to the planet on the use of quartz crystals and gemstones for the purpose of healing and alignment.

Dow crystals help you align with Christ consciousness and Buddha consciousness due to their configurations' geometric and numerological significance. Christ consciousness restores complete balance and invokes the ability to fulfill the highest potential of the current human incarnation. Aligning with the seven-sided faces of a Dow crystal aids in balancing all seven chakras. This alignment allows ascended awareness to flow through the three-sided faces to strengthen and support your connection with the trinity of body, mind, and spirit, or, from the Christian perspective, Father, Son, and Holy Spirit. In Native cultures, the Trinity might be equated to Father Sky above, Mother Earth below, and the place of the heart within, where we are all connected.

Meditate with a Dow crystal to awaken a connection with higher consciousness. This crystal is ideal when you wish to channel information from an angel, spirit guide, ascended master, or loved one on the other side.

Double Terminated Point

A double terminated point is a crystal that is terminated on both ends. Energy can be either sent or received with this type of crystal. Double terminated points are useful to move energy between two different areas. For example, placing a double terminated point between two chakras moves the life force and allows the vibration of chakras to communicate and align with each other.

If you desire to bring more love from the heart chakra to the solar plexus for self-empowerment, place a rose quartz gemstone on the heart and a citrine gemstone on the solar plexus with a double terminated clear quartz point in between the two. The quartz point amplifies the inherent love within the rose quartz and the intrinsic courage within the citrine.

Elestial Quartz Crystal

Elestials are mysterious and sacred stones. Most elestials are smoky or clear quartz crystals with multiple terminations; however, some are citrine, amethyst, ametrine, clear quartz, or rose quartz.

Elestials are etched and have many layered markings on and within them. They are fully terminated, with multiple triangular configurations around and throughout. They will help you connect and make contact with buried emotions in a way that is powerful yet not traumatic. In addition, they assist in washing away the emotional blocks that prevent you from moving forward.

The legend associated with elestials is that they were brought from Heaven to Earth by the Elohim. *Elohim* is a plural Hebrew name for God. In this context, I refer to the Elohim as the group of angels closest to God that can still reach human consciousness. The Elohim are also known as the Shining Ones or the Watchers. There is a direct correlation between these beings and their association with the messenger angels and archangels. They are sometimes referred to as the "Els." Have you ever noticed that the names of most angels ends in "el," including the word "angel" itself? Here are a few angels' names that end in -el: Michael, Raphael, Uriel, Gabriel, Raziel, Zadkiel, and Chamuel. These Elohim are the crystal guardians of the elestials.

As the Elohim brought the elestials through the dimensions, they were singed and transformed, revealing a skeletal triangular structure. Because of the angelic vibration associated with this crystal, use it to effectively connect with the legions of angels available to you.

Herkimer Diamonds

Herkimer diamonds grow in Herkimer, New York, in the Adirondack mountain range. Although they aren't actual diamonds, they are much harder than regular quartz, closer to diamonds. The measurement for gemstone hardness is called the Mohs scale, a rating system that scores the hardness of the stone on a scale from one to ten. Diamonds are the hardest, at 10, and Herkimers are 7.5.

Herkimers are double terminated quartz crystals believed to be more than 500 million years old. Most Herkimers have eighteen faces: six triangular faces form the two terminations and six squares or rectangles make up the sides of the crystal. They are most often double terminated unless a termination is broken during the mining process. Carbon inclusions (small internal fractures) are often found within Herkimers, giving some specimens a more smoky appearance. Smaller Herkimer diamonds attach to larger ones like a barnacle and when a little Herkimer has fallen off, you can see an indentation where it was attached.

Herkimers are harder to mine than many other crystals because they grow inside dolomite limestone formations, created when surface water containing high degrees of silicone seeps into dolomite limestone. Over years of intense pressure, crystals form within these limestone pockets. If you plan to mine these gems, take your hammer and chisel and align with the vibration of the seven dwarves—perhaps sing a bit, as they did!

These crystals are brilliant and sparkly. They bring more joy and clarity into your life. Their many inclusions allow light to refract and create rainbows. Because of their brilliance, they are also good magnifiers of intention.

Here is a paradox: Herkimers really move energy and are good for dreaming. However, if you use them for dreaming, you may have problems sleeping because their energy is so lively. The vibration of Herkimers reminds me of Mexican jumping beans. Don't worry, though, the vibrant energy the crystals provide keeps you conscious enough to dream lucidly.

There was a period of time when I kept a Herkimer on my nightstand with the intention of remembering my dreams. I woke up often during the night and wrote down my dreams, but after several nights, I realized I was exhausted. Once I moved the Herkimer out of the room, I slept well again. Use Herkimers to get yourself moving, but avoid them when you need restful sleep! Now I only use a Herkimer occasionally, one night at a time, when I need or want clarity through dreams.

Isis Crystal

Isis crystals are beneficial for hospice workers or people that birth people into the next dimension. The transition from this reality to the next is paralleled only by the birth into this reality. These are the two biggest changes that you go through as a human. Throughout your life you have many transitions. The Isis crystal can assist in making those changes with grace and finesse.

An Isis point helps you focus during times of change. Use the Isis crystal when you go to a school for the first time, get married, have children, get divorced, lose a friend or family member, change careers or residence, or establish a new way of being.

Isis crystals are distinguished by their five-sided faces. In numerology the number five indicates change and supports freedom and versatility. Use the Isis crystal to assist you in living outside the box and changing your patterns and behavior to realize your fullest potential.

Laser Wand "Singing" Crystals

Most laser wands are mined in Brazil. They're usually wider on the bottom or base of the crystal and then narrow to a laser point at the tip. Lasers often have etchings on the sides of the crystal and irregular lines on the sides of the point.

Lasers are used for psychic spiritual healing and surgery. Unless you have the gift of spiritual sight to clearly see the auric field, you should avoid using them for psychic surgery. You can use lasers to maintain focus during meditation.

Laser wands are usually singing crystals, as they make a sound when gently touched against each other. The gentle, tingling sound softly and subtly realigns your consciousness.

Phantom Quartz Crystals

Phantom quartz crystals have the ghostlike appearance of another crystal within them. The apparition within the crystal helps you remember who you truly are and where you are about to go. Phantom crystals help you realize you have much more to learn and opportunities from which to grow.

A phantom crystal is beneficial when you think you are advanced. In those moments, without squashing your self-esteem and positive energy, a phantom can help you look deeper to help you stretch into situations to reach your full potential. Use phantom quartz to help you stay in touch with awareness that there is always much more to know and learn. It can activate the courage to step into life situations to catapult you to your next level.

Phantom quartz is relatively rare. I come across them every so often. I've seen phantoms within clear quartz, citrine, and smoky quartz. When you come across one, pay attention and be sure you are ready to step more fully into yourself.

Record Keeper Crystals

Record keeper crystals hold records and information. You have a chance to tap into the information stored within your cells, bones, muscles, and DNA, as well as an opportunity to access the akashic records using a record keeper.

The record keeper will download what you need to know or integrate. You may or may not be cognizant of the download and in fact, it's more common to be unaware. Interestingly, however, you can instantly retrieve data from it when you need it. A good analogy is a downloaded program or a file that has been saved onto your computer's hard drive. Perhaps initially, you don't know how to use it or don't need the program or file right away. But with the passage of time and integration of knowledge, you can open, read, and use the program or file.

Similarly, record keeper crystals offer the same potential. When you meditate with a record keeper crystal, it downloads information; however, you may not know specifically what information has been downloaded. The information is retrievable when you need it. A perfect example is the information I've shared on the akashic records. It just poured through me as if I were downloading information. Up until the moment I started writing, I hadn't consciously thought of it. It flowed through me as a stream of consciousness in the moment I needed to pass the information to you.

You can identify record keeper quartz crystals by the little triangles, both faint and pronounced, etched into their faces. These etchings are naturally occurring and are not the result of human alteration. Sometimes you may have a crystal for years and never notice triangular markings on it. Bright, refracted light may reveal these triangles on the faces of a record keeper. Some crystals have hieroglyphic-like markings on the sides. They hold records, but aren't record keeper crystals per se.

Relationship Crystals

A relationship crystal is actually two crystals that grow together and share a common side. Some relationship crystals have one point that is substantially bigger or taller than the other. A crystal with this configuration may set up a vibration in which one partner could be overbearing or overpowering to the other in the relationship. This configuration may be beneficial, however, for a parent-child or teacher-student relationship.

In a twin crystal, the height of the two crystals is equal. This is the ideal in a business partnership, platonic friendship, or romantic relationship. Use the crystal with the intention to maintain a balanced, healthy, equal relationship.

A family crystal is one that has two points equal in size (as in a twin crystal) representing the parents, and one or more smaller crystals attached, representing the babies or children. The smaller attached points are usually connected at the base or on the sides of the twin, creating a cluster of crystals.

Self-Healed Crystals

Self-healed crystals have multiple triangular formations on the end of the crystal where it has broken from the main cluster. The place where the point broke off from the matrix continued to grow and heal over, forming natural triangular facets. This crystal helps heal trauma by reminding you to heal yourself from within to create a new, beautiful you.

Single Terminated Point

Simply put, when a crystal has only one termination, it is called a single terminated quartz point. The energy of this crystal is directed through the single termination. The faces of the crystal form the termination. A single terminated point can also be a channeling crystal, a record keeper, an Isis, or window crystal, to name a few. As you read further, you will find out more about these and other types of crystal points. Every natural quartz point has six sides and faces.

Tabular Faden Crystals

Tabular quartz crystals, often called tabbies, are good for communication, including telepathic linking. Telepathic linking is heart-to-heart and mind-to-mind communication. People in telepathic connections can finish each other's sentences, communicate with a glance, and telephone a moment or two before the other was about to call.

Tabbies are the marriage counselors of the gemstone world because they help you actively engage in good communication. The key to any good relationship is the ability to communicate well and truly listen. When you know you're being heard and can speak your truth, you can relax. There are many types of relationships, including the one with yourself. Tabbies assist in honesty and living your truth.

Many tabular quartz crystals have a Faden line going through them. A Faden line looks like a thin, white, fuzzy wire running through the crystal point. This line further activates the wiring for good communication.

These little, flat tablet-shaped crystals have a protective quality about them. Tabbies keep you grounded, even though they're energetically "zippy." In one way, these crystals take you to the outer limits of your consciousness while simultaneously maintaining a good connection to Mother Earth.

Tabular quartz can be easily identified: two of the crystal's sides are much wider than the other four. They easily transmit the language of light with the conscious intent of the user. The language of light is symbols, images, sounds, and words used to communicate the energy of higher consciousness.

Time Link Crystal

Unlike the perfect diamond-shaped face of a window crystal, a slightly angled parallelogram identifies it as a time link crystal. The time link face can be angled toward the right or left. Time links can assist you in mental time travel, or, in other words, projecting consciousness backward or forward through time.

To identify the type of time link, hold the face of the crystal toward you. If the parallelogram angles toward the right, it's useful for a future life progression. If the parallelogram is angled to the left, use the crystal to spiral your consciousness into a past life. Of course, to have this experience, you must use intention to aid in the meditative experience. Place the crystal on your chest or in your hand.

Because you live your life in a linear reality, you perceive the presence of time. On a quantum level, however, there is no time and no space. All potential or simultaneous realities exist in the quantum state. You have the ability to move forward in time to look at these potential realities. And likewise, you can also go back into past lives, or even your past in this lifetime, to observe and connect with experiences. This includes not only what has literally occurred, but also situations you created in your mind.

Window Crystals

Window crystals are used to look into the soul. Use a window crystal to practice self-observation. It aids in the realization of the intention behind the intention—helping you know your true essence beyond the illusions and masks you wear. Window crystals help you look inside yourself. They magnify your ability to see the mirrors or reflections offered to you daily by the people around you. You can learn many lessons as you observe the actions of others. See them as reflections of yourself. Window crystals help you observe thoughts, patterns, and behaviors and to be open to releasing some of them to realign with a higher consciousness.

The distinctive quality of a window crystal is the additional diamond-shaped face on the point. True window crystals are relatively rare. I have only come across a handful in the past twenty years.

You may think you have a window crystal, but after examining it more carefully you will probably determine that it is a time link crystal. The perfect diamond-shaped face is the defining character-istic of a window crystal, whereas a time link crystal has a slightly skewed parallelogram.

———

As you can see, the quartz family of gemstones provides the full light spectrum to activate the memory of our own rainbow body. Use these sparkling treasures of the earth to bring forth joy, hap-piness, and balance in your life. Indeed, life's geometry is found within these crystals to help you find the way on the different paths presented every day. Connecting with the geometrics of these gem-stones somehow helps our relationships interconnect with one an-other and everything! Delve into the points, shapes, triangles, win-dows, and rainbows of quartz. Let the light shine brightly on your path.

Appendix

REFERENCE CHARTS

*T*hese reference guides succinctly sum up the information throughout this book. Use this section to help refresh your memory and look up something quickly. Also, remember to use your own intuition and keep in mind that this is simply a guide.

TABLE A.1. REFERENCE CHART FOR SOUND, COLOR, STONES, AND OILS ASSOCIATED WITH EACH CHAKRA

Chakra	Note	Color	Primary Stones	Complementary Stones	Essential Oils
7 Crown	B	gold, violet, white	amethyst, apophyllite, clear quartz, selenite	apophyllite, kyanite, lapis lazuli	benzoin, frankincense, helichrysum sandalwood
6 Third Eye	A	indigo	blue sapphire, charoite, lapis lazuli, sodalite, sugilite	apophyllite, amethyst, selenite	frankincense, grapefruit, helichrysum, lavender, sandalwood, peppermint, rosemary
5 Throat	G	pastel blue or turquoise	amazonite, angelite, aquamarine, celestite, turquoise	amazonite, angelite, aquamarine, blue lace agate, turquoise	Auntie M's Anti, eucalyptus, lemongrass, tea tree
4 Heart	F#	green, pink	green aventurine, green jade, green tourmaline, emerald, rubillite, rose quartz, watermelon tourmaline, kunzite	garnet, green calcite, pink calcite, rhodochrosite, rhodonite, ruby	lavender, jasmine, neroli, rose
3 Solar Plexus	E	yellow	citrine, golden calcite, tiger's eye, yellow topaz, yellow tourmaline	amber, amethyst, apatite, malachite, peridot, prehnite,	anise, bergamot, fennel, lemon
2 Navel	D	orange	amber, carnelian, honey calcite, orange calcite, red goldstone, red jasper, tiger's eye	azurite, chrysocolla, malachite turquoise, unakite	orange, clary sage, Euphoria blend, jasmine, peppermint, rose, sweet marjoram, ylang ylang

Chakra	Note	Color	Primary Stones	Complementary Stones	Essential Oils
1 Root	C	red	black tourmaline, garnet, hematite, ruby, smoky quartz	amethyst, clear quartz, lapis lazuli, pyrite, sodalite	patchouli, spikenard, vetiver

TABLE A.2. CHAKRA EVALUATION TABLE: BALANCE AND BODY PARTS

Chakra	No.	Balanced	Out of Balance	Areas of the Body
Root	1	abundance, earth connection, focused, grounded, physical energy, survival, vitality	agitated, angry, can't achieve goals, depression, feels unloved, lacks confidence, weak, inflammations	blood, male reproductive system, nervous system, spine, testes, vagina
Navel	2	creative, optimistic, intuitive, self-motivated, sense of belonging	aggressive, buries emotions, distrustful, emotionally explosive, manipulative, oversensitive, self-negating, self-serving	female reproductive organs, kidneys, mammary glands, skin
Solar Plexus	3	ability to set boundaries, cheerful, enthusiastic, expressive, high self-esteem, mental clarity, self-confident, self-respect, personal power, relaxed	demanding, difficulty breathing, confused, feel that others control your life, inferiority complex, lacks confidence, judging, overly intellectual, poor digestion	adrenals, breath, diaphragm, digestive organs, skin
Heart	4	balanced, Christ consciousness, Buddha consciousness, compassion, empathetic, friendship, kindness, divine love, nurturing, romantic love, sees good, tolerance	abandonment issues, afraid of letting go, afraid of being free, afraid of getting hurt, controls with money, demanding, feels unworthy of love, indecisive, moody, overcritical, paranoid, possessive	heart, immune system, lungs, lymph glands, thymus
Throat	5	communication, centered, content, expressive, good timing,	arrogant, can't relax, devious, dogmatic, inconsistent, scared, self-righteous, too talkative or too quiet, timid, unreliable	eyes, ears, muscles, nerves, throat, thyroid

Chakra	No.	Balanced	Out of Balance	Areas of the Body
Third Eye	6	channel, charismatic, intuition, psychic, telepathy	afraid of success, authoritarian, egomaniac, manipulative, nonassertive, oversensitive to the feelings of others proud, schizophrenic	brain, ears, eyes, pineal gland, pituitary gland
Crown	7	access to subconscious, miracle worker, open to the Divine	can't make decisions, catatonic, frequent migraines, frustration, no joy, unrealized power, psychotic	brain, ears, eyes, pineal gland, pituitary gland

Table A.3. An A–Z Gemstone Guide to Conditions and Intentions

Condition	Recommended Stones
Abundance	citrine, emerald, green aventurine, green tourmaline, jade, pyrite
Abuse	chrysocolla, rose quartz, smoky quartz
Angel communication	angelite, celestite, elestial crystal, turquoise
Anger	chrysocolla, lapis lazuli, sodalite
Arthritis	carnelian, copper, malachite, rose quartz
Ascended masters	amethyst, cathedral library quartz, channeling quartz, kyanite, record keepers, selenite
Blood pressure	hematite, sodalite, lapis lazuli
Cancer	chrysocolla, rhodochrosite, rose quartz
Childbirth	bloodstone, carnelian, hematite, rose quartz
Communication	amazonite, aquamarine, tabular quartz, turquoise
Creativity	calcite, carnelian, orange
Digestion	apatite, citrine, prehnite, peridot
Electromagnetic frequencies	black tourmaline, fluorite
Emotional balance	lepidolite, rose quartz, rhodochrosite, unakite
Energy	Herkimer diamonds, rutilated quartz
Fertility	carnelian, hematite
Focus	fluorite, hematite, smoky quartz
Grounding	agates, black tourmaline, smoky quartz, lapis lazuli
Headaches and migraines	lapis lazuli, sodalite
Higher consciousness	amethyst, clear quartz, elestial quartz, kyanite, record keepers, selenite, vogel-cut crystal
Honesty	amazonite, turquoise
Hyperactivity	hematite, pyrite, smoky quartz
Inflammation	chrysocolla, lapis lazuli, sodalite
Intuition	amethyst, clear quartz, lapis lazuli

Condition	Recommended Stones
Intuitive development	amethyst, apophyllite, cathedral library quartz, clear quartz, kyanite, selenite
Jealousy	peridot, prehnite, tiger's eye
Love	emerald, rose quartz, rhodochrosite, rubellite, watermelon tourmaline
Meditation	amethyst,clear quartz, selenite
Menopause	chrysocolla, lapis lazuli
Mental imbalances	charoite, lepidolite
Muscles and bones	calcite, selenite
Negativity	black tourmaline, black onyx, smoky quartz
Passion	garnet, ruby
Relationships	rose quartz, tabular quartz, relationship twin quartz
Self-esteem	citrine, golden calcite, yellow topaz
Setting boundaries	amber, citrine
Sobriety	amethyst
Study	clear quartz, tabular quartz
Transformation	amethyst, charoite
Travel	aquamarine, green aventurine
Weight issues	amethyst, apatite, citrine

References

Adams, John. *The Crystal Sourcebook: From Science to Metaphysics.* Edited by John Milewski and Virginia Harford. 1st ed. Santa Fe: Mystic Crystal Publications, 1987. [*Author's Note:* This book includes information about Marcel Vogel's experiments with crystals.]

Allen, Paula Gunn. *Spider Woman's Granddaughters: Traditional Tales and Contemporary Writing by Native American Women.* New York: Ballantine Books, 1990.

Andrews, Ted. *Animal Speak: The Spiritual and Magical Powers of Creatures Great and Small.* St. Paul, MN: Llewellyn Publications, 1993.

————. *Animal-Wise: The Spirit Language and Signs of Nature.* Jackson, TN: Dragonhawk, 1999.

Bach, Edward. *The Essential Writings of Dr. Edward Bach: The Twelve Healers and Heal Thyself.* United Kingdom: Random House, 2005.

Bach, Edward, and F. J. Wheeler. *The Bach Flower Remedies.* New Canaan, CT: Keats, 1997.

Braden, Gregg. *The Science of Miracles: The Quantum Language of Healing, Peace, Feeling, and Belief.* DVD. Carlsbad, CA: Hay House, 2009.

Caddy, Eileen. *The Spirit of Findhorn.* Findhorn, Scotland: Findhorn Press, 1994.

Castaneda, Carlos. *The Active Side of Infinity*. New York: HarperCollins, 1998.

———. *The Art of Dreaming*. New York: HarperCollins, 1993.

———. *A Separate Reality: Further Conversations with Don Juan*. New York: Penguin, 1988.

———. *The Teachings of Don Juan: A Yaqui Way of Knowledge*. Berkeley: University of California Press, 2008.

Cunningham, Scott. *Magical Aromatherapy: The Power of Scent*. St. Paul, MN: Llewellyn, 1995.

Day-Schmal, Linda. *Soul-Birthing: How to Choose, Attract and Influence the Soul of Your Baby before Conception or Birth*. Sante Fe: SpiritPassage, 1997.

Emoto, Masaru. *The Secret Life of Water*. Translated by David A. Thayne. New York: Atria Books; Hillsboro, OR: Beyond Words, 2005.

Freidel, David, Linda Schele, and Joy Parker. *Maya Cosmos: Three Thousand Years on the Shaman's Path*. New York: William Morrow, 1993.

Gardner-Gordon, Joy. *Color and Crystals: A Journey through the Chakras*. Feasterville Trevose, PA: Crossing Press, 1988.

Hay, Louise. *Heal Your Body*. Carlsbad, CA: Hay House, 1984.

Hidell, Al, and Joan d'Arc. *The New Conspiracy Reader: From Planet X to the War on Terrorism; What You Really Don't Know*. New York: Citadel Press, 2004. [*Author's Note:* This book includes information about Marcel Vogel.]

Javane, Faith, and Dusty Bunker. *Numerology and the Divine Triangle*. Atglen, PA: Schiffer, 1979.

Luminare-Rosen, Carista. *Parenting Begins Before Conception: A Guide to Preparing Body, Mind, and Spirit for You and Your Future Child*. Rochester, VT: Healing Arts Press, 2000.

Marciniak, Barbara. *Earth: Pleiadian Keys to the Living Library*. Rochester, VT: Bear & Company, 1995.

Mead, Jerry D. "Wine on the Rocks" *International Wine Review.* February/March 1989.

Melody. *Love is in the Earth: A Kaleidoscope of Crystals; The Reference Book Describing the Metaphysical Properties of the Mineral Kingdom.* Wheat Ridge, CO: Earth-Love, 1991.

Milanovich, Norma, and Shirley McCune. *The Light Shall Set You Free.* Scottsdale, AZ: Athena, 1996.

Miller, Hamish, and Paul Broadhurst. *The Sun and the Serpent.* Hillsdale, NY: Pendragon Press, 1989.

Ouspensky, P. D. *In Search of the Miraculous: Fragments of an Unknown Teaching.* New York: Harcourt Brace Jovanovich, 1949.

Raphaell, Katrina. *Crystal Enlightenment: The Transforming Properties of Crystals and Healing Stones.* Vol. 1. Santa Fe: Aurora Press, 1985.

———. *Crystal Healing: The Therapeutic Application of Crystals and Stones.* Vol. 2. Santa Fe: Aurora Press, 1987.

———. *Crystalline Transmission: A Synthesis of Light.* Vol. 3. Santa Fe: Aurora Press, 1990.

Sellar, Wanda. *The Directory of Essential Oils.* Saffron Walden, UK: C. W. Daniel, 1992.

Shinn, Florence Scovel. *The Writings of Florence Scovel Shinn.* 4th ed. Camarillo, CA: DeVorss, 1996.

Snider, Jerry, and Richard Daub. "The Advocacy of Marcel Vogel" *Magical Blend: A Transformative Journey Magazine,* 1989. [*Author's note:* I have a copy of this magazine article with the cover, but I am unable to see a volume number or a clear date published.]

Spero, Maria. *Chichen Itza: A Guide to the Ruins.* Self-published, 1990.

———. *Exploring the Yucatan Peninsula.* Self-published, 1995.

———. *Uxmal.* Self-published, 1995.

Stearn, Jess. *Edgar Cayce: The Sleeping Prophet.* New York: Bantam, 1989.

Stein, Diane. *The Women's Book of Healing.* St. Paul, MN: Llewellyn Publications, 1987.

Sugrue, Thomas. *There Is a River: The Story of Edgar Cayce.* Virginia Beach, VA: A.R.E. Press, 2003.

Taylor, Terry Lynn. *Messengers of Light: The Angels' Guide to Spiritual Growth.* Tiburon, CA: HJ Kramer, 1989.

Tompkins, Peter. *The Secret Life of Plants.* New York: Harper, 1989.

Valentine, Tom. "Marcel Vogel: The Man Who Would See Magnetism." *Magnets in Your Future.* June 1986. Volume 1, no. 6, page 3.

Virtue, Doreen, and Lynnette Brown. *Angel Numbers: The Angels Explain the Meaning of 111, 444 and Other Numbers in Your Life.* Carlsbad, CA: Hay House, 2005.

Waters, Frank. *Book of the Hopi.* New York: Penguin, 1977.

White Eagle. *Spiritual Unfoldment 2.* 2nd ed. Camarillo, CA: DeVorss, 2008.

Worwood, Susan. *Essential Aromatherapy: A Pocket Guide to Essential Oils and Aromatherapy.* Novato, CA: New World Library, 1995.

Yogananda, Paramahansa. *Autobiography of a Yogi.* 2nd ed. Nevada City, CA: Crystal Clarity, 2005.

INDEX

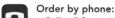
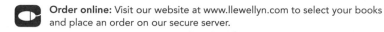

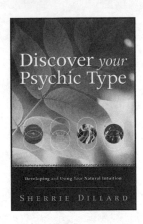

DISCOVER YOUR PSYCHIC TYPE
Developing and Using Your Natural Intuition
SHERRIE DILLARD

Intuition and spiritual growth are indelibly linked, according to professional psychic and therapist Sherrie Dillard. Offering a personalized approach to psychic development, this breakthrough guide introduces four different psychic types and explains how to develop the unique spiritual capabilities of each.

Are you a physical, mental, emotional, or spiritual intuitive? Take Dillard's insightful quiz to find out. Discover more about each type's intuitive nature, personality, potential physical weaknesses, and more. There are guided meditations for each kind of intuitive, as well as exercises to hone your psychic skills. Remarkable stories from the author's professional life illustrate the incredible power of intuition and its connection to the spirit world, inner wisdom, and your higher self.

From psychic protection to spirit guides to mystical states, Dillard offers guidance as you evolve toward the final destination of every psychic type: union with the divine.

978-0-7387-1278-9
288 pp., 5³⁄₁₆ x 8 $15.99

CHAKRA HEALING AND KARMIC AWARENESS
KEITH SHERWOOD

Accumulating karmic baggage—the dense energy carried from one lifetime to another—is a common hazard for many. This debilitating energy can negatively influence one's personality, relationships, physical health, and spirituality.

The author of *Chakra Therapy* offers a step-by-step approach to overcoming karmic baggage and energy blockages. Keith Sherwood's easy techniques can help you activate the chakras, strengthen boundaries (the surface of auras), arouse the kundalini, and embrace personal dharma. He also teaches how to take care of your energy system and condition it for physical, mental, emotional, and spiritual well-being.

978-0-7387-0354-1
312 pp., 6 x 9 $14.95

EVERYDAY CLAIRVOYANT

Extraordinary Answers to Finding Love, Destiny and Balance in Your Life

CYNDI DALE

This engaging book from professional clairvoyant and best-selling author Cyndi Dale features true personal stories and practical advice on how to handle everything from everyday concerns to major life decisions. Cyndi has provided intuitive consulting and healing to more than thirty thousand individuals, helping them lead more successful, happy, and prosperous lives. In this fascinating book, she shares what she's learned with readers in a fun Q & A format that is organized into three categories: relationships, work or destiny, and health. Heartwarming, humorous, and surprisingly down to earth, *Everyday Clairvoyant* also shows readers how to develop and make use of their own intuitive gifts.

ISBN-13: 978-0-7387-1923-8
312 pp., 5¾₆ x 8, $16.95

THE PURSUIT OF HAPPINESS
Integrating the Chakras for Complete Harmony
DAVID POND

Many people today need guidance in finding fulfillment in our often-disconnected world. Human beings are complex, but the secret to experiencing happiness is simple—you need only to look within.

David Pond, author of the bestselling *Chakras for Beginners*, offers an easy-to-follow system for manifesting true happiness in your life. Pond describes all seven dimensions from which we experience life—physical identity, emotions, willpower, heart center, thought patterns and intuition, imagination, and spirituality—and gives practical methods for developing and integrating all levels. Focus your attention, seek clarity with meditation and breathing, ground your energy, fine-tune your emotional intelligence, cultivate stronger relationships—and much more.

Transcending religion and accessible to everyone, this seven-step program shows you how to overcome everyday challenges, achieve a healthy balance, be a better partner and friend, and create a richer and fuller life.

ISBN-13: 978-0-7387-1403-5
264 pp., 5³⁄₁₆ x 8, $15.95